SAY UNCLE!

SAY UNCLE!

CATCH-AS-CATCH-CAN WRESTLING
AND THE ROOTS OF ULTIMATE FIGHTING,
PRO WRESTLING, & MODERN GRAPPLING

• • • • JAKE SHANNON • • • •

ECW

Published by ECW Press
2120 Queen Street East, Suite 200, Toronto, Ontario, Canada M4E 1E2
416-694-3348 / info@ecwpress.com

LIBRARY AND ARCHIVES CANADA CATALOGUING IN PUBLICATION

Shannon, Jake
Say uncle! : catch-as-catch-can and the roots of mixed martial arts, pro wrestling, and modern grappling / Jake Shannon.

ISBN 978-1-55022-961-5
Also issued as 978-1-55490-961-2 (PDF); 978-1-55490-946-9 (EPUB)

1. Wrestling—History. 2. Mixed martial arts—History. I. Title.

GV1195.S536 2011   796.8'12   C2011-900890-4

Editor for the press: Michael Holmes
Cover Design: David Gee
Text Design and Typesetting: Marijke Friesen
Production: Rachel Ironstone
5

PRINTED AND BOUND IN CANADA

ECW PRESS
ecwpress.com

DEDICATION

This book is dedicated to the memory of my friend Karl Gotch
and to my best teacher in grappling, Mr. Billy Robinson.

GRATITUDE

TEACHERS/COACHES
Billy Robinson, Dick Cardinal, Karl Gotch

ATHLETES
Josh Barnett, Yoshiaki Fujiwara, Tom Puckett, Frank Shamrock,
Wade Schalles, Mark Schultz, Gene LeBell, Mark Fleming, Frankie
Cain, Erik Paulson, Dan Severn, Billy "Pops" Wicks, Harry Smith,
Brandon Ruiz, Neil Melanson, Randy Couture, and Sam Kressin

WRITERS AND HISTORIANS
Bob Calhoun, C. Nathan Hatton, Mike Chapman,
Mark Hewitt, Mark Jones, Scott Teal, and Liza Joseph. Special
thanks to Robert Red-Baer, who helped to translate my interview
with Yoshiaki Fujiwara, and to my friend, my training partner, and
an all-around grappling genius, Brandon Ruiz for sharing some
of his "buddy" weight conditioning ideas with me.

FAMILY AND FRIENDS
Sondra Shannon, Gil Shannon, Joey Senter, Jesse Marez, Drew Price,
David Zorn, Christopher Morsey, Gene and Ted Pelc, Ryan Hanlon,
Bill Cogswell, Phil Friedman, Odis Meredith, Brian Yamasaki, Glenn
Ortiz, Brandon Kiser, Gerald Harris, Kris Iatskevich, Russ Jensen,
Mark "Samohi" Black, John Fabbricatore, and John Fitzgerald

TABLE OF CONTENTS

PART 3
TECHNIQUES • 149

CONCLUSION • • • • • • • • • • • • • • • • • • • 203

CATCH-AS-CATCH-CAN LEXICON • • • • • • • • • • • • 205

★ ★ ★ INTRODUCTION ★ ★ ★

THIS BOOK IS THE CULMINATION of a decade-long firsthand study of the sport, science, and art of catch-as-catch-can wrestling from tough, dangerous old-timers like Billy Robinson, Karl Gotch, Dick Cardinal, and others. Though I do not claim to be a catch-as-catch-can guru, fans of my website, ScientificWrestling.com, know the care and dedication I've poured into sharing what I've learned about this amazing sport. In fact, any real contribution I've made to catch-as-catch-can lies in my leadership, research, and organizational and pedagogical skills rather than any athletic prowess. My research for this book was shaped by my extensive first-hand experience with top catch-as-catch-can men from yesteryear, as well as with those modern practitioners who trace their training lineage back to the old catch wrestling style. I've done my very best to rely on primary, independent sources. This book represents my latest understanding and knowledge of catch-as-catch-can and supersedes everything else I have written on the subject.

For those unfamiliar with the sport, catch-as-catch-can wrestling is, first and foremost, a set of rules for grappling competition: 1) you win with a submission or pin, 2) there is no point system to determine a winner, and 3) the winner is declared after the best two of three falls. As a martial art, catch-as-catch-can is a rich, colorful style in which each practitioner expresses the art uniquely. It is efficient, brutally painful, and seeks to maximize the use of balance, leverage, and metabolic conditioning. Its three fundamental rules make catch-as-catch-can exciting and entertaining for participants and spectators alike. Clarence Eklund explains the rules of catch-as-catch-can thus:

> A fall is gained when both shoulders of one wrestler touch the ground together, and very seldom are falls registered from standing throws. This necessitates most contests being completed on the ground or mat. Much of this ground work is admittedly very skillful. No kicking, striking, or other foul activities are permitted, but theoretically every hold is legitimate. Exceptions are made of strangle holds or others designed to cut off an opponent's breathing, and those grips or forms of attack which cause acute pain or are intended to force the defender to roll on his shoulders to avoid injury by dislocation or fracture.[1]

Because of its rules, catch wrestling focuses primarily on ground wrestling. Although rules existed on paper for professional wrestling matches, referees generally exercised considerable discretion and would allow a liberal amount of "roughing." There is no "takedown" point system to speak of, and it is impossible to pin someone while standing. It may also be less likely to secure a submission win while standing, though it's not impossible, so catch wrestlers seek to use gravity as an offensive weapon. As catch wrestling legend Karl Gotch used to say, "bulls get killed on the floor." The catch-as-catch-can man is confident when taking a fight to the ground, knowing gravity is on his side. When the match goes to the ground, the catch wrestler can deftly change from being as light as necessary, in order to transition from position to position, to being incredibly heavy, thereby making his opponent fully carry his weight as he effectively controls and subdues his opponent. As

---

1 Quoted from Clarence Eklund, *Wyoming's Wrestling Rancher: Life and History of Clarence Eklund, Champion Wrestler* (Buffalo, H.H.E. Odegard, 1993), 25.

in modern mixed martial arts (MMA), a catch-as-catch-can man can "tap out" to concede, or he could concede to a submission by rolling onto his back.

For many, catch wrestling has been more than a set of rules; it's an institution, a lifestyle even. I cannot resist quoting here the words of Sir Thomas Parkyns from *The Inn-Play or Cornish Hugg Wrestler*:

> Some perhaps may object, that Wrestling is no use, but apt to make a Man more Contentious and Quarrelsome, and fit only to break Men's Bones; to which I answer, that you seldom find a Gamester indeed, but is superlatively passive, and will put up with what another shall call and resent as an affront; neither do you find that a true Gamester does, or receives any Harm, but when highly provoked. Instead of a true Gamester being Contentious and Quarrelsome, he'll laugh at small Indignities, and as with the Mastiff Dog, rather than bite, lift up his Leg and only piss upon the little wafling yelping Curs in Contempt.[2]

In many ways, catch wrestling embodies the cultural values prevalent at the turn of the 20th century, which may explain why its popularity peaked at that time. The sport expressed the values of independence, reason, hard work, and competitiveness in various ways.

INDEPENDENCE Catch wrestling is not a team sport. One man stands alone atop the mountain of beaten and broken competitors to be crowned champion. The catch wrestler understands that he alone is responsible for his successes and his failures.

REASON Catch wrestling is a dangerous game of physical chess. The terms "science" and "scientific" are frequently used in the context of catch

---

2 Sir Thomas Parkyns, *The Inn-Play or Cornish Hugg Wrestler 1727* (Buffalo: H.H.E. Odegard, 1993).

wrestling. It's the smart player who's rewarded, not necessarily the strongest.

HARD WORK Catch wrestlers didn't have cushy mats. During the American Civil War they competed on grassy fields. After the war they'd compete on gravel-covered clearings following a full day in coal mines or steel mills. During the height of its popularity, with the likes of Tom Jenkins, George Hackenschmidt, and Frank Gotch, catch wrestlers competed on hard floors covered only in canvas. Wrestling is hard. It takes a special person to show up at the gym, day after day, year after year, and push beyond his physical and mental limits.

COMPETITIVENESS These men were filled with pride and were motivated to prove their skills. They would bring an equal purse to each match and the winner would take all—meaning they literally put their money where their mouths were, and were always game.

The aim of this book is to share the history and strategies of old-time catch wrestlers with today's grapplers and encourage the evolution and development of the modern sport of catch wrestling. I also hope to awaken fans of fighting sports to the fact that catch-as-catch-can is, arguably, the direct ancestor of today's mixed martial arts, pro wrestling, and Olympic freestyle wrestling. In fact, the term "no-holds-barred" was coined to promote early 20th century American catch-as-catch-can wrestling matches. If you enjoy the Ultimate Fighting Championship (UFC), the WWE, Olympic or collegiate freestyle wrestling, or high school folkstyle wrestling, you owe an enormous debt of gratitude to catch wrestling.

★ ★ ★ PART I ★ ★ ★
A HISTORY OF CATCH-AS-CATCH-CAN

THERE HAS BEEN WRESTLING in some form or another as far back as recorded history goes. The walls of the Egyptian temple tombs of Beni Hasan, near the Nile, are painted with hundreds of wrestling scenes that illustrate a great number of the holds and falls known today.[3] Wrestling was a very important branch of athletics in ancient Greek games. In fact, it formed the chief event of the pentathlon. There were two basic types of Greek wrestling—upright wrestling, which was most common, and *lucta volutatoria*, which took place after the takedown and continued until one of the contestants conceded to the other. Greek upright wrestling was not unlike modern Greco-Roman wrestling; however, three falls out of five decided the winner of the match. The upright wresting was also employed in *pankration*, a brutal combination of boxing and wrestling similar to today's mixed martial arts contests. No holds were barred.

---

3 See Nat Fleischer, *From Milos to Londos: The Story of Wrestling Through the Ages . . .* (New York: The Ring Inc., 1936), 2.

Both the Saxons and the Celts adored grappling, and English literature abounds with references to it. King Henry VIII was known to have been an especially powerful wrestler.

The Americas have a strong wrestling heritage that predates European colonization. Native American tribes had been wrestling for hundreds of years before settlers arrived, in a style somewhat similar to judo. The Native American wrestler won by throwing his opponent, rather than by pinfall, as we see in modern wrestling.

In the fledgling United States, President George Washington was renowned in colonial Virginia for his prowess in the Cumberland-and-Westmoreland wrestling style. Abraham Lincoln was legendary in rural Illinois for his long string of victories in the collar-and-elbow style of wrestling (developed in the New England farming country). American colonial and frontier wrestlers practiced styles derived from English wrestling. The three major styles were named after the English counties where they were developed: Cumberland and Westmoreland, Cornwall and Devonshire, and Lancashire. The Cumberland-and-Westmoreland style was a Greco-Roman-like style and the aim was to throw the opponent while maintaining a solid over/under hold. The Cornwall-and-Devonshire-style wrestlers wore jackets not unlike those worn for judo and jujitsu, and they were allowed to grab onto these harnesses. Early forms of Cornwall-and-Devonshire were exceptionally brutal and allowed combatants to wear boots reinforced with steel toes and soles, which they used to kick each other until one man gave up. The last, Lancashire catch-as-catch-can, was loosely based on Greek *pankration* and is the forerunner of modern freestyle amateur wrestling, mixed martial arts, and even staged pro wrestling.

Though some speculate it began in Ireland, the precise beginnings of catch-as-catch-can wrestling are not really known. The first recorded matches contested under its rules—submission or pin wins the match; best two of three falls with a win, lose, or draw format; and no points—began appearing in the English county of Lancashire at the dawn of the Industrial Revolution. The name "catch-as-catch-can" is a Lancashire phrase that simply means "catch me if you can." The men were tough—wrestling each other on gravel after a long day spent working in a coal mine—and often wrestled for money, putting side bets on their matches. Eventually, some of these men earned enough money from these side bets to make a living from wrestling alone, and so the modern professional competitive wrestler was born.

As the sport of catch-as-catch-can grew in popularity, it followed immigrants from England and the rest of Western Europe to the United States. As a true workman's sport that required little, if any, expensive equipment, catch wrestling spread like wildfire among the bored soldiers of the American Civil War.[4] By the end of the 19th century, Americans were so enamored of catch-as-catch-can that contests attracted large paying crowds and championships and titles were instated.

The first big wrestling celebrity in America was Evan "The Strangler" Lewis (not to be confused with the later champion Ed "Strangler" Lewis). He was notorious for using the strangle hold to win his matches. The strangle wasn't always an illegal maneuver, but it eventually fell out of public favor as a result of its frequent use. The popularity of catch-as-catch-can wrestling grew over the decades, eventually generating millions of dollars. Predictably, with the money came corruption. Greed led the promoters and competitors of the day to fix fights. This ultimately led to a crisis of confidence, and professional wrestling stopped being a competitive sport and became the performance art we see on television today.

However, there were those who kept the sport of catch-as-catch-can alive. In the United States, prior to television and amusement parks, traveling carnivals were a popular form of entertainment. These carnivals often employed wrestlers who would take on all comers. Since carnival wrestlers didn't know whom they would be facing day to day, they needed to know how to wrestle and protect themselves legitimately. Fortunately, some carnival wrestlers, men like Dick Cardinal and Billy

---

4 See Nat Fleischer, *From Milos to Londos: The Story of Wrestling Through the Ages . . .* (New York: The Ring Inc., 1936), 19.

Wicks, kept the little-known techniques alive and taught them to new generations of wrestlers.

Carnival wrestlers were not the only ones who had an interest in keeping catch wrestling alive, though. There were professional wrestlers trained in the Lancashire birthplace of catch-as-catch-can, in Wigan, a town in Greater Manchester, in northwestern England. Two of the most outstanding athletes from there (and I am lucky to say I call them "friend") are Billy Robinson and Karl Gotch. They aren't just the most influential wrestlers to have trained in Wigan, they are arguably the most influential of the catch-as-catch-can men of their era. Their efforts to keep competitive catch-as-catch-can alive culminated in the very first and largest modern mixed martial arts promotion.

THE INFLUENCE OF CATCH-AS-CATCH-CAN ON MIXED MARTIAL ARTS

Mixed martial arts competitions, for the few who may not be familiar with the sport, give martial artists from different traditions and backgrounds the opportunity to test their strengths in competition. It allows striking and grappling, both while standing and when on the mat. However, what you may not know is that the first modern match between a striker and a grappler happened all the way back in 1887, between heavyweight boxing champion of the world John L. Sullivan and Greco-Roman wrestling champion William Muldoon. It ended with Sullivan being slammed to the mat and incapacitated. The next big mixed match of this kind took place in the late 1890s, when boxer Bob Fitzsimmons challenged European wrestling champ Ernest Roeber. Roeber took Fitzsimmons to the mat and applied an arm lock, making Fitzsimmons quit. In 1936, heavyweight boxer Kingfish Levinsky challenged professional wrestler Ray Steele in a mixed match that saw Steele win in just 35 seconds.

They were all proving a point, which casual MMA fans might have thought started with Royce Gracie in the early 1990s: grappling is a powerful form of martial arts. However, serious students of Western combat sports know that catch-as-catch-can men were twisting up their opponents like balloon animals decades before Gracie jujitsu was even a twinkle in Carlos or Helio Gracie's eye. Karl Gotch learned catch-as-catch-can submission maneuvers from old-timers like Billy Riley and Joe Robinson at the Snake Pit gym in Wigan, England, and from Americans like Frank Wolf, Ben Sherman, and Ed Lewis. These men learned from the generation before them. Karl Gotch would later go on to influence the generation of Japanese fighters that would start the very first mixed martial arts promotions. Yoshiaki Fujiwara, Masakatsu Funaki, and Minoru Suzuki all learned the methods and techniques of catch-as-catch-can directly from Karl Gotch. They, in turn, influenced the styles of many American MMA champions, such as Ken and Frank Shamrock.[5]

More than 10 years Karl's junior, Billy Robinson, another dangerous wrestler from the Snake Pit gym, would go on to become perhaps the most successful catch-as-catch-can trainer in MMA history. The legendary fighter Kazushi Sakuraba, known widely in Japan as the "IQ Fighter" and the "Gracie Hunter," credits Billy Robinson as being the trainer who most influenced his incredible submission grappling skills. Robinson has also taken king of Pancrase and the youngest UFC heavyweight champion in history Josh Barnett, a winner of numerous submission grappling tournaments, under his wing. Barnett wins his MMA fights with submissions, like the toehold, which have traditionally been associated with competitive catch-as-catch-can wrestling matches from the early 20th century. Most recently, Robinson's coaching and insights into submission grappling have been sought out by legendary UFC hall of famer Randy Couture and his head grappling coach, Neil Melanson

---

5 See Jonathan Snowden, *Total MMA: Inside Ultimate Fighting* (Toronto: ECW Press, 2008), 59. The book presents an in-depth chronology of the expansion of MMA, from its beginnings until late 2008.

(whose first exposure to catch-as-catch-can came from the teachings of Gene LeBell).[6]

For many, modern MMA began in 1993, with Ultimate Fighting Championship, an MMA promotions company based in the United States. The very first UFC tournament gave wide exposure to the power of submission grappling, when Royce Gracie subdued three challenges within just five minutes. However, this was not the first mixed-styles match of its kind, not even for the Gracie family. Royce's father tangled and drew with catch-as-catch-can men Fred Ebert and Wladek Zbysko decades earlier.

The jujitsu/catch-as-catch-can rivalry goes back to even before the Gracie family got involved. Mitsuyo Maeda, the man who (under the moniker Count Koma) introduced jujitsu to the Gracie clan in Brazil, is said to have honed his personal combative style while competing in catch-as-catch-can wrestling tournaments at the turn of the last century. It was during this time that Maeda perfected his unorthodox method of fighting while lying on his back. However, in the mid-1990s, while catch-as-catch-can was languishing in obscurity in the United States, the Gracie style of jujitsu was gaining popularity due to new fighting promotions and clever booking strategies created to showcase the Brazilian martial art. However, nearly a month before the cage doors slammed shut in McNichols Arena for the first Ultimate Fighting Championship on November 12, 1993, Pancrase: Hybrid Wrestling held the first modern MMA matches in Tokyo Bay NK Hall on September 21, 1993.

The promoters of this new Japanese style were none other than Masakatsu Funaki and Minoru Suzuki, men who had learned their submission wrestling methods from both Yoshiaki Fujiwara (a tough collegiate judoka, catch-as-catch-can wrestler, and the man Antonio Inoki chose to corner him in his infamous Ali fight) and Fujiwara's guru, Karl Gotch. Unfortunately, with Pancrase fighters Ken Shamrock

---

6 See Neil Melanson, the head grappling coach at Randy Couture's fight gym, discuss the relevance of CACC to MMA here: http://www.youtube.com/watch?v=KGu4WE27DD0.

and Masakatsu Funaki eventually losing at the hands of Gracie fighters via chokes, it became clear that modern catch-as-catch-can men needed to cross-train in other martial arts to remain viable. These catch wrestlers learned about the importance of throat submissions the hard way in early MMA competitions—both how to apply them and how to defend against them. Ironically, nearly a century earlier, in Book 12 of *Lessons in Wrestling and Physical Culture*, catch-as-catch-can icon Martin "Farmer" Burns warns wrestlers about strangle holds: "In my opinion there is very little in the so-called Jiu-Jitsu teaching that is not included in a full and complete knowledge of catch-as-catch-can wrestling. There are, of course, a few holds and defenses, such as the throttle hold, the strangle hold, etc., that are not used in wrestling, yet these holds are generally understood by the thoroughly trained wrestler."[7]

He goes on to say, "The reason that Jiu-Jitsu has been so much over-rated is because the subject has been advertised and the special holds emphasized, while as a matter of fact there is very little new in the subject for anyone that has made a study of Physical Culture, Wrestling and American Self-Defense."[8]

It didn't take catch-as-catch-can wrestlers long to adapt to the demands of mixed martial arts and Brazilian jujitsu. While working for the Union of Wrestling Forces International (UWFI) promotion in Japan, Kazushi Sakuraba, a Japanese pro wrestler trained in catch-as-catch-can wrestling by Billy Robinson, soon cut through the top jujitsu players. Those that Sakuraba went on to soundly defeat read like a "who's who" of Brazilian jujitsu black belts and MMA fighters at the time: Marcus Silviera, Vitor Belfort, Royler Gracie, Renzo Gracie, Ryan Gracie, and Royce Gracie. This earned him the nickname the "Gracie Hunter" and put catch-as-catch-can squarely back on the map. Sakuraba's other nickname, the "IQ Fighter," epitomized Billy Robinson's

---

7 http://www.sandowplus.co.uk/Competition/Burns/lessons/lesson12.htm

8 http://www.sandowplus.co.uk/Competition/Burns/lessons/lesson12.htm

assertion that catch-as-catch-can wrestling is akin to "physical chess" and Karl Gotch's maxim of "adapt and improvise."

Bruce Lee, who popularized the idea of combining the elements of multiple martial arts in the United States in the late 1960s and early 1970s, believed that the best fighter was not a boxer nor a karate or judo man but someone who could adapt to any style. By adapting and improvising, catch-as-catch-can wrestling–based fighters went from being strangled by the jujitsu man's uniform (in Ken Shamrock versus Royce Gracie) to using it against them (in Sakuraba's later match against Royce). The old matches often had strangles, but the holds could be barred during match making, so as to adapt catch-as-catch-can to the modern MMA arena.

THE INFLUENCE OF CATCH-AS-CATCH-CAN ON PRO WRESTLING

American professional wrestling hasn't always looked like the McMahon family's choreographed melodrama, seen on television Monday and Friday nights. As late as the early 20th century, many matches were legitimate contests. And for the contestants of that era, wrestling was not just a sport but a science, a means of attaining superior physical fitness and a brutally efficient form of self-defense. For people like Martin "Farmer" Burns, Tom Jenkins, George Hackenschmidt, Frank Gotch, Charley Cutler, Eugene Tremblay, Joe Stecher, Waino Ketonen, Ed Lewis, and Henry Kolln, it was a way of life.

As such, sometimes the athletes forgot that the paying crowds were just as important as who won the match. For example, in a legitimate contest on July 4th, 1916, in Omaha, Nebraska, Joe Stecher and a young Ed Lewis grappled for five hours during match that, by all accounts, was excruciatingly boring.[9] While "works" (match fixing)

---

9 For more details see Tim Hornbaker, *National Wrestling Alliance: The Untold Story of the Monopoly That Strangled Pro Wrestling* (Toronto: ECW Press, 2007), 66.

had always been a part of professional sports, wrestling at the time took fixing matches to an entirely different level.

However, wrestling promoters soon realized that scripted matches with predetermined outcomes were far more profitable and generated revenue streams that were far more reliable than those associated with legitimate catch-as-catch-can contests. To exert control over any wrestler who might "shoot" (and win a match that the promoters didn't want him to win), the promoters cartelized and were thereby able to blacklist any competitive wrestler who rebelled. And so, straight contests gave way to "worked" performances, not unlike those we see on TV today. The public only caught on when sportswriters of the day busted the promoters' scam by leaking the results of these fixed contests well before they were actually held. This drove authentic competitive catch-as-catch-can wrestling in the United States underground. Interestingly enough, the rules you see on today's televised "sports entertainment" still reflect the old catch-as-catch-can rules, where a pin or submission may win the contest.

In the United States, professional wrestling, as a form of sports entertainment in which professionals wrestled for payment, originated in the 1860s and 1870s. Martin "Farmer" Burns was one of the biggest names, having fought 6,000 matches and reportedly losing fewer than 10, all the while weighing no more than 160 pounds (about 70 kg). Burns's most famous student was Frank Gotch, who is largely regarded as the greatest competitive catch wrestler ever. Gotch became the undisputed world heavyweight champion in 1908 by beating the reigning European champion, George Hackenschmidt, and successfully defended the title against him.

Unfortunately, due both to the growing suspicion regarding the authenticity of pro wrestling contests and to Gotch's retirement in 1913, the popularity of pro wrestling waned. In the 1920s, Ed Lewis, Billy Sandow, and Joe "Toots" Mondt came together to promote their own brand of wrestling, which was more entertainment than sport.[10] They introduced time-limited matches and also began retaining wrestling performers for longer periods, allowing for long-term feuds and storylines. This unique approach, along with flashy holds and signature moves, was successful enough to earn them the nickname the "Gold Dust Trio." Tim Hornbaker describes it in *National Wrestling Alliance: The Untold Story of The Monopoly That Strangled Pro Wrestling*:

> The unconventional style of working, albeit not entirely modern, was more elaborate and absorbing than the usual fare. Lewis intentionally acquired heat, and wrestling audiences cried foul when he "crippled" opponents with his headlock. The inventive angles were driving people into complete hysterics, periodically pushing crowds to the verge of rioting. Midwestern fans were just a decade removed from watching the technical performances of Frank Gotch. Now they were seeing the current champion, Strangler Lewis, purposely maiming a ring rival. Lewis was perfect as an erratic and violent wrestler, and Sandow was brilliant at the way he spun the webs.[11]

The 1930s and 1940s saw fierce inter-promotional matches in which independent wrestling companies and promotions fought to gain dominance. The National Wrestling Alliance (NWA) was formed in 1948, and Lou Thesz was chosen to bring the various championships under a single "world heavyweight" title. Before devoting the majority of his life to these worked "entertainment" matches and becoming quite possibly the most successful professional wrestler ever (with

---

10 Tim Hornbaker devotes an entire chapter to Joe "Toots" Mondt, titled "The Red-Haired Shooter," in *National Wrestling Alliance: The Untold Story of the Monopoly That Strangled Pro Wrestling* (Toronto: ECW Press, 2007), 94–108. It's a useful read and provides some additional context.

11 Tim Hornbaker, *National Wrestling Alliance: The Untold Story of The Monopoly That Strangled Pro Wrestling* (Toronto: ECW Press, 2007), 68.

respect to both earnings and longevity), Thesz had briefly learned the ropes from some of the toughest and meanest competitive catch-as-catch-can men around, like George Tragos and Ad Santel.[12] However, by the time Thesz was just 21 years old, he was the world champion in the highly protected, controlled, and politicized arena of professional wrestling, his competitive catch-as-catch-can days cut tragically short by the seductive money and fame offered by the new "performance art" style of professional wrestling. On December 29, 1937, Thesz was thrust into the world spotlight by "beating" "Colorado" Everett Marshall in a predetermined match.[13]

Had a promotion like the Ultimate Fighting Championship been around in their day, this author is confident that many of the toughest "entertainment" wrestlers of the time, men like Karl Gotch, Billy Robinson, Thesz, George Gordienko, Dick Hutton, and Danny Hodge, would have not only participated in it, but most likely dominated it.

Unfortunately, there was no such organization. Many who had proven their mettle in amateur wrestling or other sports found that the only way they could continue doing what they loved and put food on the table was to compromise by performing instead of competing.

By the time pro wrestling began airing on television in the 1950s, and its popularity exploded once again, anything resembling a legitimate wrestling contest was gone, and the focus had turned entirely to entertaining, but preordained, outcomes. Interestingly, before the World Wrestling Federation (now known as World Wrestling Entertainment, having lost a trademark case brought by the World Wildlife Fund) came to dominate professional wrestling, the competitive spirit of old-school catch-as-catch-can would occasionally resurface here and

---

12 See Lou Thesz and Kit Bauman, *Hooker: An Authentic Wrestler's Adventures Inside the Bizarre World of Professional Wrestling* (Seattle: TW-Press Book, 2001) for more details.

13 You'll find more on Thesz's early entry into the world of pro wrestling in Lou Thesz and Kit Bauman, *Hooker: An Authentic Wrestler's Adventures Inside the Bizarre World of Professional Wrestling* (Seattle: TW-Press Book, 2001), 76.

there. In 1963, professional wrestler and amateur judo champion Gene LeBell accepted a challenge to fight high-ranking middleweight boxer Milo Savage in Salt Lake City, Utah. LeBell choked Savage unconscious in the fourth round. Thirteen years later, Gene LeBell, as referee, found himself in the middle of perhaps the most famous such encounter, this time between boxing icon Muhammad Ali and Karl Gotch–trained professional wrestler Antonio Inoki.

With Gotch-trained Yoshiaki Fujiwara in his corner, Inoki intended to shoot on (that is, wrestle competitively with the intention of winning) the legendary Ali, hoping to yet again demonstrate the superiority of catch-as-catch-can over boxing. Ali's camp thought it was going to be a fake fight, a joke, and realized only upon arrival in Tokyo that "no one was laughing."[14] Learning of the competitive intentions of Inoki's camp, Ali's camp insisted on a drastic change to the rules of engagement—just two days before the scheduled event. Originally Ali was to follow traditional boxing rules with Inoki being expected to stay within the bounds of traditional professional wrestling rules. The new set of rules effectively neutered any wrestling that Inoki might have employed, barring throws, tackles, submissions, and any kicks that did not have one knee on the mat. In Karl Gotch's words, the event was an "abortion," ending in a draw after 15 rounds. Ali was able to throw only six punches and ended up in the hospital with legs full of hematomas. Under the revised rules, Inoki had resorted to scooting around on the ground and viciously kicking Ali's legs.[15]

Within a decade, wrestling in the United States and Japan began to flirt with honesty, albeit in completely different ways. By the 1980s, the WWF had nearly become the monopoly it is today, and Vince McMahon, its owner, legitimized the scripted outcomes by openly admitting to the theatrics. He even coined the term "sports entertainment" to more accurately describe what was being aired. In Japan, however,

---

14 See also http://www.thesweetscience.com/boxing-article/1716/joke-almost-ended-ali-career.

15 See http://www.thesweetscience.com/boxing-article/4326/talking-boxing-angelo-dundee/ for additional details.

this flirtation with honesty manifested itself in a slow weaning from predetermined outcomes and a move toward increased levels of realism. Japanese promotions, such as the Universal Wrestling Federation (UWF), the Professional Wrestling Fujiwara-Gumi, the UWFi, Fighting Network RINGS (RINGS), Shooto, and Pancrase, were inspired and pushed by the likes of Karl Gotch and Billy Robinson and began to slowly "revolutionize" professional wrestling by bringing it full circle, back to its competitive catch-as-catch-can roots.

THE INFLUENCE OF CATCH-AS-CATCH-CAN ON FREESTYLE WRESTLING AND MODERN SELF-DEFENSE

Just as the discipline of judo was born when Jigoro Kano removed the dangerous maneuvers from jujitsu to create a safer sport, amateur freestyle wrestling was born when the more dangerous holds and submissions were removed from professional wrestling. Like Greco-Roman, freestyle is not only a popular style of modern competitive wrestling, but also an Olympic sport.[16] However, unlike Greco-Roman, freestyle wrestling allows the attacking of the opponent's legs in offense and defense. "Win by pin" is the target of the freestyle wrestler; however, in the absence of submissions, an elaborate point system may also determine the winner. Freestyle wrestling was introduced in the Olympics in 1904 (with all 40 participants being American) and has been there ever since.

Seeking first-hand knowledge of how useful grappling can be in hand-to-hand combat, President Theodore Roosevelt appointed former American catch-as-catch-can wrestling champion Tom Jenkins as the head self-defense instructor at the Military Academy at West Point. Both President Dwight D. Eisenhower and General George Patton

---

16 See also http://www.olympic.org/en/content/Sports/All-Sports/Wrestling/Wrestling-free-style/Wrestling-freestyle-Equipment-and-History/?Tab=1.

learned hand-to-hand from Jenkins.[17] In Jenkins's words, "There ain't no hold that can't be broke," as there aren't any rules that can't be broken. Amateur freestyle wrestling can be turned into a devastating form of self-defense by systematically breaking Articles 52 and 55 of the International Federation of Amateur Wrestling (FILA) rules[18] (I have edited the articles for brevity):

ARTICLE 52—GENERAL PROHIBITIONS

Wrestlers are forbidden to:

★   pull the hair, ears, genitals, pinch the skin, bite, twist fingers or toes, etc. and generally, to perform actions, gestures or holds with the intention of torturing the opponent or making him suffer to force him to withdraw

★   kick, head-butt, strangle, push, apply holds that may endanger the opponent's life or cause a fracture or dislocation of limbs, tread on the feet of the opponent or touch his face between the eyebrows and the line of the mouth

★   thrust the elbow or knee into the opponent's abdomen or stomach, carry out any twisting action which is likely to cause suffering, or hold the opponent by his singlet

★   cling to or grasp the mat

★   talk during the bout

★   seize the sole of the opponent's foot (only seizing the upper part of the foot or the heel is permitted)

★   agree the match result between themselves

ARTICLE 55—ILLEGAL HOLDS

The following holds and actions are illegal and strictly prohibited:

★   throat hold

---

17 You'll find this information in Mike Chapman, *The Life and Legacy of Frank Gotch: King of the Catch-as-Catch-Can Wrestlers* (Boulder: Paladin Press, 2008), 14.

18 http://www.fila-wrestling.com/download/rules_jan2005.pdf

★   twisting of arms more than 90 degrees

★   arm lock applied to the forearm

★   holding the head or neck with two hands, as well as all situations and positions of strangulation

★   double Nelson, if not executed from the side without the use of the legs on any part of the opponent's body

★   bringing the opponent's arm behind his back and at the same time applying pressure to it in a position where the forearm forms an acute angle

★   executing a hold by stretching the opponent's spinal column

★   chancery hold with one or two hands in any direction whatsoever

★   the only holds allowed are with the head and one arm

★   in standing holds executed from behind when the opponent is head down (reverse waist hold), the fall must be executed only to the side and never from top to bottom

★   in executing a hold, only one arm may be used to hold the opponent's head or neck

★   to lift the opponent who is in a bridge position and then to throw him onto the mat (severe impact on the ground); that is, the bridge must be forced down

★   breaking the bridge by pushing in the direction of the head

★   generally, if the attacking wrestler is found to have violated the Rules during the execution of a hold, the action in question shall be completely void and the wrestler at fault, penalized (caution). If the attacker repeats his violation, he will be punished by a caution. One point will be awarded to his opponent.

These rules inform you of which moves and holds are deadly. Breaking the rules delivers a very effective self-defense system since, in real life-and-death situations, there are no rules.

Bearing this context in mind, it's worth recounting the story of Imi Lichtenfeld. Lichtenfeld developed street fighting skills to defend himself against anti-Semitic activists in Bratislava in the 1930s. His father was a carnival wrestler and acrobat, and, later, a police officer. He passed his passion for grappling, athletics, and self-defense to his son, Imi. Imi would later become a champion wrestler, winning the Slovakian youth wrestling championship in 1928 and the adult welterweight championship in 1929, a time when the terms "amateur wrestling" and "amateur catch-as-catch-can" were interchangeable. In the same year, he also won the national boxing championship and an international gymnastics championship. After immigrating to Israel, Lichtenfeld provided hand-to-hand combat training to what later became the Israel Defense Forces (IDF).

This system of training would eventually become known as krav maga, a system similar to catch-as-catch-can in its aggressiveness and brutality. (Having undergone intensive basic krav maga instructor training at the Krav Maga Worldwide facility in San Antonio, Texas, I can personally vouch for this similarity.) Krav maga applies striking techniques and weapon disarms to real-world self-defense situations. Training typically involves high-stress street patrol or combat situations designed to inoculate practitioners against the effects of stress on fine motor skills. Learning to ignore distractions, developing a keen awareness of potentially dangerous situations, dealing with potentially violent situations, and learning ways to avoid violence when possible are all part of the training. Today, krav maga has become commercially successful and is still used by IDF special forces units, and variations of krav maga are used for civil and military purposes in several parts of the world.

Catch-as-catch-can wrestling has played a crucial role in the development of modern mixed martial arts, sports entertainment and WWE-style wrestling, Western close quarter combatives, and freestyle and folkstyle wrestling. Now, let's talk with some of the men who were crucial in keeping catch-as-catch-can alive.

★ ★ ★ PART 2 ★ ★ ★
INTERVIEWS: THE ORAL HISTORY OF CATCH-AS-CATCH-CAN

OVER THE YEARS, through a combination of good fortune, persistence, and research prowess, I've been able to pick the brains of some of the true masters of catch-as-catch-can wrestling. On the following pages you'll find highlights of conversations that convey their experiences, their wisdom, and their techniques—what made them wrestlers to reckon with. The pieces on Karl Gotch, Billy Robinson, and Dick Cardinal capture personal conversations and the convivial time I got to spend with them. (The transcripts included herein are abridged, but I hope to someday provide the full audio versions online).

The interview with Billy Wicks captures his extraordinary experiences from his time wrestling in carnivals and as a professional wrestler and as a law enforcement officer. Frankie Cain takes us through his wrestling career and gives us glimpses into his contemporaries, along with some rarely retold firsthand accounts of wrestling and wrestlers.

The interview with Fujiwara, Karl Gotch's best student, reveals a balanced, thoughtful personality. He talks about his life, his training, and his philosophy. The multitalented Gene LeBell has a ton of excellent, and often hilarious, tidbits to share. Josh Barnett gives us a quick overview of the world of MMA and pro wrestling, and he discusses his mission to restore catch to its rightful place in the world of professional fighting. Mark Fleming, Lou Thesz's only protégé, talks about his wrestling journey and his close personal relationship with Lou.

In all of these interviews you'll find these luminaries talking about how they met the challenges they faced, not just as men but as wrestlers.

★ ★ ★ KARL GOTCH (1924–2007) ★ ★ ★

IN GRAPPLING, THE NAME KARL GOTCH is even more imposing than his towering physical presence. Wrestling took him from Belgium to England to Germany to the United States and to Japan, making him well known for his formidable metabolic conditioning and knowledge of submission grappling. He wrestled in the 1948 Olympic Games in London, representing Belgium, just a few years after he nearly died in a Nazi concentration camp in Poland. It was in England that Alf Robinson (wrestling promoter and uncle of catch-as-catch-can legend Billy Robinson) invited Karl to Billy Riley's gym in Wigan, England. There, Karl was introduced to submission grappling, the hard way, and subsequently he became dedicated to learning the ropes of catch-as-catch-can wrestling from the likes of Joe and Bob Robinson. (The latter was also known as Billy Joyce, and neither brother was directly related to either Billy or Alf Robinson.)

Karl stayed in England for years, studying the craft, the science, and the art of the physical chess game that is catch-as-catch-can wrestling. He later built a reputation as a shooter—a dangerous wrestler with few peers—in the scripted and hyper-politicized world of professional wrestling. Long on competitive ability but short on charisma, Karl was eventually marginalized by American promoters, especially after incapacitating the then National Wrestling Alliance heavyweight champion, Buddy Rogers, during a locker-room dispute in the fall of 1962.

Rogers filed assault charges, and both Karl and his friend "Big" Bill Miller were picked up (and later released on bond) by the Franklin County, Ohio, sheriff's department. Fortunately, Miller would prove to be far more than just a fighting buddy. Facing a hard time and unable to find wrestling work in the United States, Karl received an invitation from Miller to wrestle with him in Japan. It was in Japan, as Antonio Inoki's teacher, that Karl Gotch would earn his moniker the "God of Wrestling."

In 2003, while researching reliable catch-as-catch-can resources, I stumbled upon Karl's contact information. I wrote him a letter and described my obsession with and vision for catch-as-catch-can, never really expecting a reply. To my surprise, in August 2003 I received a call from him. I was shocked. In stark contrast to his reputation for being a bit of a curmudgeon, I found Karl to be very open and funny. I found that if you were honest and sincere in your attempt to learn from him, he was very giving. So much so that sometimes I couldn't get him to stop! Fortunately, I recorded dozens of hours of these phone conversations, spanning 2004 to 2007.

Over the Christmas holiday of 2005, while visiting family in Florida, I was able to spend a few days with Karl. He answered the door wearing his exercise jumpsuit and a big smile. With a glass of red wine and a cigar in hand, we settled down on his patio and talked wrestling for the next hour and a half.

A few laughs later, Karl looked at me very seriously. "Jesus," he said. "Look at your neck. You look like one of the guys that were at the concentration camp with me during World War II. You got these big muscles everywhere, but your neck looks like a goddamn pipe cleaner! You come all this way here from California! You got to let this old man show you a thing or two!"

Karl didn't know about my neck problems from having received radiation treatments as a teenager fighting cancer (Hodgkin's disease), and I didn't want to waste Karl's time with all of that. So after a huge cigar and a glass of wine (on an empty stomach), faster than you could say "Great Gama," Karl had me out doing one of his insane conditioning workouts.

He started me out twirling his Indian clubs (both the gada and the jori), which was no easy feat since each weighed about 20 pounds (10 kg)![19] Afterward, it was some Hindu push-ups and half-moon push-ups. I think he was a bit surprised when I fell into a wrestler's bridge from standing. After a few more exercises, Karl was kind enough to show me a few toehold submissions, the crooked leg scissor, and some takedowns.

The next day, at a steakhouse and over some prime rib, Karl got to talking about the history of the sport, especially about *Catch: The Hold Not Taken*, a DVD I'd sent him so I could get his perspective on it. While he enjoyed the footage and the fine directing, he felt that proper respect had not been given to the American catch-as-catch-can style.

> America had the best catch men in the world. Everyone knew that. Maybe now, some of the old-timers tell you this and that, but believe me, I have nothing to gain saying this . . . I remember Old Man Riley came over to the United States to wrestle once. Well . . . he was back in Wigan even before he left! He never ever talked about it after he came back. Of course, America had all the best catch men—men like Frank Wolf, Fred Grubmeyer, John Pesek, Ad Santel, Toots Mondt, and the grandaddy of them all, Strangler Lewis.

---

19 This experience with the gada led me to bring the Macebell to life. See www.Macebell.com.

Lancashire style came to America from England. Everybody from around the world brought a little from each of their countries to form the American catch-as-catch-can style. The American style was unbeatable by anyone on the planet.

Well, back then, the Americans, when they went to Europe, they all went to Paris. Not London, not Prague, not Frankfurt. The Americans all wanted to go to the City of Lights. This is why the French had such great catch-as-catch-can wrestling at the time. When FILA first started, they had three styles—freestyle, Greco, and amateur catch-as-catch-can.

Our talk rambled along the alleys of American wrestling history interspersed with interesting tidbits and the critique of the DVD.

Robert Arnaud had a good school. He had a student, a guy named Leduc, who was good too, although he had been mouthing off that he had taught old Ben Sherman a lesson. Well . . . Ben showed up at his gym looking to wrestle. Leduc left before Benny could even lace up his boots. He left so quick that he left his street clothes behind!

What also was amazing [in the DVD] was that there was hardly any mention of Riley's pistol man, Joe Robinson. Old Joe Robby took a liking to me and showed me the ropes. He was the best one there, not Riley. Riley was a businessman. Now, Riley could wrestle, but he was by no means the best one there.

There was also no mention of the man who taught Riley, the Irishman "Pops" Charnock. He was a real tough one . . .

Our conversation continued for the rest of the afternoon. The day after Christmas, we met up again.

This time when I knocked, all I heard was a stern "Come in." He was sitting at his desk with a deck of cards. I knew then that I was in for Gotch's Bible.

Here's how you do it: shuffle a full deck of cards (jokers included). Every time you deal a black card you have to do squats—regular Hindu squats for spades and jump squats for clubs—double the amount of the face value of the card. That is, if you get a black 8 you do 16 squats, and if you get a black ace you do 22. Red cards represent push-ups, and you have to do the actual face value of the card—regular Hindu push-ups for diamonds and half-moon push-ups for hearts. And so, if you get a red 8 you do 8 push-ups, and if you get a red ace you do 11. With only eight cards left I could do no more. My legs simply would not go. I was huffing and puffing harder than I ever have on a treadmill, and I'm in good shape. Well, this woke me up to what a *real* workout feels like.

"I used to do this twice in a row," Karl said with a laugh. No wonder he was such a terror on the mat. He *always* had gas in the tank. Karl passed away in August 2007, and I was given the honor, by his estate, of breaking the news to the world. He was my friend and is sorely missed.

★ ★ ★ BILLY ROBINSON (1939–) ★ ★ ★

IN MY ROLE AS a sort of "Johnny Appleseed" of catch wrestling, I have had the great fortune of being able to pick the brains of high-level practitioners like Karl Gotch, Yoshiaki Fujiwara, Dick Cardinal, Billy Wicks, Josh Barnett, and scores of others. On the morning of March 28, 2007, I went to LAX to pick up Billy Robinson and began learning from arguably the greatest competitive catch-as-catch-can coach of modern times. Born in 1939, Billy, like Karl Gotch before him, learned at Billy Riley's gym in Wigan, England, and traveled the world wrestling both competitively and as a performer. Before recently relocating to the United States, Billy had coached for years at Miyato's Universal Wrestling Federation (UWF) Snake Pit gym in Japan. Before that, Robinson was the grappling trainer for the Union of Wrestling Forces International (UWFI), where he coached perhaps his most infamous pupil, Kazushi Sakuraba.

After having spent most of our first day together talking about wrestling, its history, and so on, on the second day of my visit we went to the Santa Monica High School wrestling room (where I had been coaching on weekends) and put on our wrestling shoes. We had about 10 people present, and Billy ran us through conditioning drills like Hindu squats, bar muscle-ups, pulling (a.k.a. pummeling), and more. This was an extra-special clinic, attended by MMA stand-out Josh Barnett, WWE superstar (and son of "The British Bulldog" Davey Boy Smith) Harry "DH" Smith, and Erik Paulson, a shooto light heavyweight champion and big-time MMA trainer. Several Japanese athletes participated in Billy's second clinic the next day, including Megumi Fujyii and Hiroyuki Abe. Billy covered maneuvers that are seldom seen. There was a novel counter to the double wristlock that I imagine both Renzo and Royler Gracie would have liked to have known before facing Kazushi Sakuraba. The third day of training ended with some great food, great drink, and great conversation at Jerry's Famous Deli in Marina Del Rey.

I've spent time with men like Yoshiaki Fujiwara, Karl Gotch, and Dick Cardinal, but this time I knew I had found a man who had had great success not only as a practitioner, but also as a coach. These were the first of hundreds of hours that I would be lucky enough to spend under Billy Robinson's watchful eye, learning the art and science of real catch-as-catch-can wrestling. The greatest thing about Billy, in my mind, is that not only is he a world-class athlete and coach, he is also an intellectual and an avid learner:

> . . . [Wrestling] is a control thing. Once you learn it and you learn how to learn, you never stop. Believe me, it is the greatest sport in the world. Once you get into it, it will be with you for your whole life . . . It's like riding a bike. Once you learn it, you just know how to ride the bike. Once you learn how to wrestle, you never forget . . . With catch-as-catch-can wrestling, the major thing is to learn how to learn. Once you get that, once your coach, like Jake or myself or

some other old-timer, has got into your mind how you can learn, you never stop learning. I'm learning now because, with this mixed martial arts, there are different situations, so I see it, and then it doesn't take long to figure out how to counter it. I'm learning it because I never came across that situation. But because I've learned how to learn, I have no problem with it or teaching somebody how to beat it . . . So, that's my answer. It's just great. Once you learn how to learn, it just mushrooms out.

Billy's expertise covers not just the techniques of catch-as-catch-can, but its history as well.

Wrestling was always a big sport in Europe for thousands of years. You get tournaments going back over 2,000 years that I know of. And the thing is, when these seamen [the British Navy] went to different countries—and every country had its own style of wrestling—they picked up the best of all the different styles, going back to William, and Wigan made it scientific . . . Okay, let me explain this. Gotch was in the 1948 London games and was a wrestler from Belgium. My uncle saw him. At the time, my uncle was wrestling in Antwerp, Belgium. He went over, and he saw Karl. He had seen him in the Olympics. My uncle invited him over to Wigan. At Wigan, 145-pound [65-kg] guys were beating him with submissions. He couldn't believe it. So he left Belgium, came and lived for three or four months in my uncle's house. Then he went to Wigan, which is 26 miles [42 km] away, and lived there for five or six years. And that's where he learned how to wrestle. All these great catch wrestlers in Japan get their style from the Wigan style of wrestling.

Billy Robinson had spent eight years in the tough training environment of the legendary Snake Pit at Wigan.

At Wigan, intially, you're not shown too much, and you are used as a sparring partner, but the coach watches you. Like in my case, it was close to four months before he said, "Okay. We'll start to teach this kid." They wanted to make sure I would stay, stick it out, no matter what happened to me. And that's what they did. Not just for me. With everybody . . . Once you do that, like the old-timers you practice with, guys you could learn how to beat, they still like it when they beat you. "He's a piece of shit" or "He's no good," that never happened. You respected them by just getting on the mat. And later on, when you're that much better, they're going to hope you would help them out. The respect is there with anybody, no matter how low or how high, because you know that nobody will say, "I am this. I am that." That will never happen because there's always somebody that will knock the shit out of you.

Unfortunately, there's very little of that breed now, in the youth today. With the old-timers, there was no Internet, computers, telephones, clubs, no social life. There was no distraction. Then, nobody had any money, so all the youth of all the countries were full of vim and fire. And they wanted to do something, so they'd join a soccer or rugby club or judo, jujitsu, boxing, and, the toughest of all, catch-as-catch-can wrestling, submission wrestling. And you had many, many sparring partners because it was just hundreds of guys around, in every town.

But the old-timers used to come down to the gym because of the atmosphere. And if they see you do something wrong, after your training session, they'd pull you to one side, explain to you, show you, get you back on the mat with a different sparring partner, and make you do it. And the thing was, I used to wake up with [my] head up, screaming, because I'd hear this voice, Billy Riley's voice, Karl

Gotch's, God . . . screaming at me, "Do it again. Do it again."
And I'd wake up with ringing in my ears, "Do it again. Do
it again."

If you want to be a martial artist, you've got to put the
time in, in the gym, on a lot of the disciplines or whatever
style . . . It's so much to be a showman. Everybody reacts
differently. The reflex system is different. Some people are
loose limbed. Some people are stiff. Some people are very
strong. Some people are very fast. And you've got to learn
how to make any move or any position. Work with anybody. And the only way to do that is to learn your body
precision: how to get power from the alignment of knees,
head, shoulders, ankles, toes, and heels so that you can get
the most powered speed from your own body to be able to
achieve a situation where you can do anything with anybody.

You don't fear anybody in the street. Walking down
the street, if somebody tries to mug you, you know you're
going to beat him, or at least he's not going to hurt you, put
it that way. But the thing is, you cannot learn from video-
tapes, DVDs. You have to get on the mat and feel it. You
have to get the position so you learn how to get the most
out of your own body. Condition is your fuel. Your heart is
your car. The more you know of every aspect of this terrific
sport, the more chances you've got, whereas guys that know
one or two holds, they've got to wait or force a position
where they can get those few moves.

Unfortunately now, with the mixed martial arts,
they've cut the pinfalls out, which to me is terrible because
a lot of the submissions that we've learned the last two days
can be got a lot easier from somebody trying to defend himself from being pinned because, as he turns or tries to escape
from a pin, he'll leave an ankle or a loose arm or head for a
crooked head scissor or many, many things. So now you've

got to do these things, but you've got to do them from a different position, you know.

Billy is among the few catch wrestlers who have traveled the world (Europe, North America, Asia, and Oceania) and won titles nearly everywhere he's wrestled.

The European nations are so close together. You can get to all those countries, and then they all go far back. Each country has its own style of wrestling. Maybe just a little bit different in the rules, but they did their own styles. The African tribes, the Indian tribes, the South American tribes—all had their own form. That's why you go back. You can go back like 1,000 years and find hieroglyphics of wrestling . . . It's like a circle. You'll get certain holds while you're beating people back. Other people see this. They copy those holds. Then everybody's doing those holds, and they forget the other holds. And then it goes on to the next segment, and the next segment, and then they start to catch up with the holds that were being used at the other side of the circle.

One thing about this sport: we don't hide anything or don't [not] show anybody. We want you to learn it, so that once you learn it you'll like it. You're going to get into it and then form your own gym or whatever it is . . . Or just enjoy it. Once you've felt how to get the painful situations and how easy it is to get them, it's catch me if you can or catch-as-catch-can. I'm trying to catch you, and you're trying to catch me. Catch-as-catch-can. That's what it means.

★ ★ ★ DICK CARDINAL (1927–) ★ ★ ★

BORN RICHARD CARDINAL IN 1927, in Everett, Washington, Dick Cardinal began his wrestling career as an amateur at the age of 10. He is one of the few top-ranking catch wrestling hooking experts still alive. I sought out Dick Cardinal after speaking with some wrestling old-timers at a Cauliflower Alley Club hook wrestling reunion (the Cauliflower Alley Club is a fraternal order of ex-wrestlers). The following transcript is of a lengthy phone interview that Dick granted me back in 2003. Over the next few years, I was fortunate to study with him and learn first-hand his methods of carnival-style of catch-as-catch-can, which he perfected during his years as a professional carnival wrestler.

JAKE SHANNON: I would like to share your story with people who are interested in the more legit side of catch-as-catch-can wrestling, grappling, and so on. Now, you have obviously worked as a pro, but then you worked doing carnivals too.

DICK CARDINAL: I did. I worked the At Show for quite a few years. Of course, there was some working involved, but there were also some competitive matches, particularly in places like logging or mining towns or college towns. In logging and mining towns, the wrestlers weren't [*chuckle*] . . . well, they weren't that technically skilled. The college towns, of course . . . why, you had some pretty skilled amateurs that would come up.

JS: But they didn't know the hook wrestling.

DC: No, they didn't know the hook wrestling—that's where I had the great advantage. I had an amateur background, but the addition of the hooks gave me a pretty good advantage. There were other advantages too. When you are in a ring, rather than on a mat, under lights in a real dark arena, so many of them are real tight when they come in. A tight muscle wears out a lot faster than a relaxed muscle, and, also, it reacts a lot slower. So I had that advantage, and I had other things I would do. Sometimes I would want to talk or be friends, you know. At other times I wouldn't talk. I would just stare at 'em. I wouldn't say anything.

JS: Psychological kind of stuff.

DC: Yeah. You'd have a psychological advantage, and that keeps them a little tight, and then they move a little slower. Their reflexes are slower, and, of course, they are not used to any holds that aren't joint holds because they aren't allowed to use those.

In amateur wrestling, or college wrestling, the idea is to control your guy without hurting him, but with the hook wrestling, it's entirely different. You try to end the match as quickly as you can. Although a lot of times, why . . . with the guys, if they weren't real capable, we would actually carry them. For example, a lot of times, if I wasn't sure, I'd take the guy down and ride him. Just kind of wear him out a little bit, you know. I'd make sure he'd carry my body weight. I'd get a top body scissor, something where he'd be carrying my body weight. After two or three minutes of just riding him without trying to turn him or do a lot with him, I'd get him up and put my head in and under his arms. So then we'd have a headlock, and then I'd grab his hands so he had to hold onto it, and then we would work from there. You know, you'd still be in control of the match. A headlock isn't much of a hold because you're actually behind the guy, so you could control the match, but, to the crowd, it looks like he's getting you, you know. So that was part of the theme because it's a money business too, and this is in the At Shows, so you have to kind of please the crowd and make the match. But, generally, if the guy was tough I'd take him out, [*chuckling*] you know.

JS: Because you didn't even want to take the risk of like, "hey, maybe I'll stretch this out." Meanwhile he's actually a tough guy . . .

DC: Yes, exactly, yeah. And you do run into some tough guys. It's a funny thing. Let me tell you this story 'cause it's kind of a funny one. This happened in a small town up here . . . Port Townsend, and it was this young, good lookin' stud kid. I mean, he was probably about 220 [100 kg].

At the time, I was about 175–180 [79–82 kg]. He comes up out of the crowd, and, boy, talk about a following. I thought, "Geez, we're going to be wrestling a world-beater." So Sepp comes in and says, "Get rid of this guy," you know, because I was the only guy at the platform at that time that could wrestle in a competitive sense. The other two guys were both performers, or "workers." And so I went in with the guy, and I took him out quick. It was actually very simple and easy. I took him down with a head-and-arm hold. For those that aren't familiar with that, you simply shoot your right arm up past your opponent's ear from a tie-up position and try to have the deltoid of your shoulder hit him right under the nose. It drives the guy's head up, and then you just take him right to the mat with a head-and-arm hook. And as we were going down, I put a reverse arm bar on with my legs. That just means I hooked his right wrist so that I had an arm bar with my legs, so the joint of his elbow was right across my knee area. And then I took the head and pulled it one way. There was tremendous pressure on his elbow joint, and the guy hollered. And I told him to holler louder because I wanted to make sure everyone in the place could hear it.

JS: [*laugh*]

DC: So he couldn't say, "Well, I didn't give up," you know. At any rate, when we got all done with this match, which was a shoot match, [*chuckling*] why, I got out of the ring and some gal accosted me. She says, "That was the damnedest fake I have ever seen," she says. "I see real wrestling on television, you know. I'm informed."

JS: [*laugh*]

DC: So I [*chuckling*] went out and got back up on the platform outside, and then a performer from Seattle—he was working for the promoter— jumped up on the platform and pointed at me and says, "I want him." And the crowd just went bananas, you know, because they knew they'd seen this guy on TV, and, uh, I said, "I don't want nothin' to do with this guy." You know, I just finished a tough match, and, uh . . . they made the match, and, geez, we made a lot of money that day [*chuckling*].

JS: Nice. And she probably didn't even get the irony. It was probably completely lost on her.

DC: Oh no, she had no idea of what had gone on there. The match that she'd come in to see was this performer, Gordon Heffel—a very, very good professional performer. And, anyway, we had three matches. We turned the tip three different times. We tipped the matches close. I'd come out and say, "Give me one more winner with this punk, and I'll take him out of here," you know. And we turned this over, you know . . . We turned the crowd . . . Turning the tip means to get the crowd to come back in to watch the wrestling. And, uh, we turned it over three different times. So I had [*chuckling*] a heck of a payday because I had the shoot match, where I got all the money, and that was a big crowd. And then, just because of all the yelling and screaming . . . why, an additional crowd came, and when Gordon jumped up there and challenged me, and so . . . it was a very good payday that day.

JS: Now, you mentioned Sepp. You're talking about August Sepp?

DC: Yes, August Sepp.

JS: Can you tell me a little bit about him?

DC: Yeah. I'd won a wrestling tournament in Seattle called the Pacific Northwest Amateur Tournament, and in that tournament you'd get guys actually from all over the United States but, primarily, from [the] Vancouver, Canada, area, Idaho, Montana, uh . . . Oregon, and Washington, and sometimes California. Well, anyways, in this particular final match, I beat a fellow that had been five-time national champion in the 160-pound [73-kg] division, and, you know, I wasn't expected to win this. In fact, the *Seattle Post-Intelligencer* called it a stunning upset, you know. Of course, I didn't feel that way. Now, in fairness to this fellow . . . why, he'd beat me in two previous tournaments, but I was young, comin' up, and he was older, maybe going to college, you know.

JS: I see.

DC: And so, I out pointed him in this final match. Well, anyway, at the end of this, to get to the point, this old fellow with big cauliflower ears comes up and says, [*with accent*] "Kid, you wrestle good." He was Estonian and Russian, and he says, "You want to come to my gym and work out?" And I said, "Sure, I'll come." I was all pumped up, you know. Geez, I could whip anyone in the world, I thought. I went down to his gym to work out with him, and, right away, he took me down and [*chuckling*] hooked my arm and hooked my leg, so I say, "Boy, there's more to this than I realized," you know. But that's where I got my first taste of hook wrestling and commission wrestling. Him and another fellow, both were very, very good technical wrestlers. And Sepp was an extremely good hooker—a very strong guy for his size. He was about 165 pounds [75 kg]. His size belied his strength. He was just a powerful fellow and an extremely accomplished hooker. I know he couldn't work worth a damn . . . I mean, I've worked with him a couple times, but he was more like a wrestler, you know, a real push-and-tug-type match.

JS: Yeah, stiff . . .

DC: But he had wrestled with guys like Ad Santel and held his own.

JS: Wow, wow.

DC: So I know that, I mean, I can attest to the fact that he was a *very* good wrestler. And very knowledgeable. Earlier in his career he had barnstormed in Colorado . . . He was telling me about it one time. He wore a pair of shorts, and he always had a hat that came down and rested on his ears. So he looked like a rube, you know, and that's the way he would act, and he would go into these areas, where they would have a fairly decent wrestler, and he would wrestle him for a purse. Sepp was a very good wrestler and acknowledged by many of the tough pros as an extremely tough guy. There was a fellow named Hans Schmidt. The "German Oak," he was called. He came down to the gym and worked out with Sepp. He was a big fellow, about 270 [122 kg], but he couldn't beat Sepp. Sepp couldn't do a hell of a lot with him. He was just so big. But Schmidt said, "I never knew that I couldn't beat a fellow that size."

JS: Wow, pretty tough guy.

DC: Sepp was *very* tough and mentally very strong.

JS: Now, you've worked with Vic Short too.

DC: Oh yes. Vic Short . . . and Ben Sherman, another very tough guy. I'll get to Vic here in a minute, but the other guy that I want to mention here is Ben Sherman, who was an extremely tough fellow. Ben had been the 1932 national champion, and he was out of Oregon. Ben was around for a long time performing, but he was a very tough guy. I'll just give you a little hint of how tough he was. You know the story with Karl Gotch?

JS: Hmm, not sure.

DC: This was, 'course, earlier in Gotch's career. Ben had gone over to Europe, and Karl Gotch, admittedly, found out that Sherman was a tough guy. And at that time, Ben was only about 180 pounds [82 kg]. He wasn't a real big guy, but he beat Gotch . . . In fact, he beat guys all over Europe, and Ben finally headed over to England, and one of the guys said, "Well, Bert will take care of him." Bert, that is, Bert Asratti, about five-foot-six [1.7 m], 270-pound [122-kg] strong man. But, anyway, Bert couldn't beat him. Ben didn't beat Bert, but Bert could not beat Ben either.

JS: Wow . . .

DC: Ben had tremendous vitality. He never seemed to get tired. Vic Short was a guy that was a very good hooker, a guy that was always in *superb* shape. His body fat was probably around nine or ten percent. I mean, he really took care of himself and trained hard. He was very quick, like a cat, on the mat—about 180-pound [82-kg] fellow and a very good wrestler. He wrestled back in Illinois, and he lost one match as a collegian. He had a good amateur background, and he became a very good hooker.

JS: Where did he go from college?

DC: So he studied under August Sepp. Vic and myself, and sometimes Ben Sherman and another guy named Bud Anderson and another fellow . . . We would all work out together, you know, and trade off on each other, so . . . so those were some of the guys I worked out with. They were all top-notch hookers and shooters, and we were all pretty . . . [*chuckling*] pretty competitive and pretty determined, you know. No one liked to go under in front of any of the other guys.

JS: Yeah.

DC: So that, basically, was it. I don't know if you're familiar with the At Show or not, but in the At Show there would be two or three wrestlers and maybe a promoter ...

JS: And then the stick too.

DC: Beg your pardon?

JS: A stick? Isn't that what they called the guy?

DC: Oh, the guys out in the crowd?

JS: Yeah.

DC: They call him a stick or a plant—someone that would be put out in the crowd. We'd go out on the platform and kind of strut around and muscle flex and do things that, uh ... [*pause*] ... you know ... would kind of irritate the crowd a little bit. We'd go up on the platform and do other things like, well, we had a fighter that weighed about 140 pounds [64 kg], and I could elevate him overhead pretty easily. People would see that, and they'd come down, you know, 'cause, you see, someone lifting a guy over their head at that time was ...

JS: A spectacle.

DC: Yeah, exactly, and they'd come down to see what was going on, and it wasn't that tough a lift. There was a way to do it. I mean, he would keep his body stiff, and I would get him between his legs, and he'd grab my hand, and I'd get the other hand up around his chest, and he'd leap up so I could cling him pretty easily and then just push him overhead. And so we'd get the crowd. Then Sepp would get on the microphone and challenge anyone in the crowd to come up. Earlier in the week we sometimes wouldn't have a stick there. We'd just take whoever came up, so those were usually shoots. As you know, sometimes we'd carry them through ... it just depends on the situation. For example, I had a guy who was a manager of J. C. Penney and had done some wrestling earlier in his life. He paid us 50 bucks to carry him through, you know. I didn't put him over, but I'd carry him through the match, you know, so that it made him look fairly decent. And then at other times, we'd try to get the shooters to come out, and we'd knock them off 'cause that meant good money for us, and it also paved the way for Friday and Saturday, which were the big nights, and a lot of times the local promotion would send out a boy . . . so you had some good guys to work with. Otherwise you'd have, maybe, what we'd call crowbars, the guys that were real stiff, hard to work with. So that was basically what the At Show was like. Much different then . . . It was a lot of fun . . . Why, I really enjoyed it [*chuckle*].

JS: A lot different than the kind of scene being a professional wrestler.

DC: In the At Show, matches were geared for 10, 11, 12, 15 minutes. And you had to move pretty fast, you know, because you're trying to kind of sell this thing and get them excited so they go out and scream and yell and attract other people off the midway. But you had to control the crowd, the heat, you know, the anger, so that they wouldn't get so mad they'd tear the place down. It could happen, so there was a kind of balance, but the thing that I remember the most was we moved pretty fast . . . There was constant action. In pro matches, sometimes some of the guys were kind of sluggish, and you could have a good match without doing a lot of fast movement, you know, a good performance match. They were just slower, and some of the guys just weren't in as good a shape as some of the guys [*chuckling*] that worked in the athletic show. In the At Show matches, we'd have, maybe, a 10-minute match, but it'd be a lot of movement. And then we'd have, you know, 20 minutes later another hard, fast movement, another 10-minute match like that—maybe 8 to 10 of those through the day. So we're used to moving fast. I had to slow it down a little bit when I started working more pro matches.

JS: Now, obviously you guys wrestled a ton, especially back in the At Show time. I'm a little bit curious as to what else you guys did to keep in shape and make sure you had good wind and so on.

DC: The workouts you mean?

JS: Yeah.

DC: Both Vic and I were very conscious about staying in shape, so we would run, we would do hill running, and we would spend time in the ring. This was all during the days before the At Show even opened. And we would do some lifting, primarily of sandbags. We didn't carry weights with us, so we'd just get some bags, fill 'em with dirt, and use 'em to do leg squeezes. We'd lift these bags, like weight lifting.

JS: And those probably mimicked the weight of a human body better than a barbell anyway.

DC: Yeah, exactly. In weight training, why, a lot of times you work in a certain plane, and the workouts that we did, I would say, were more like a multi-angular type of lifting. No one is going to lay still while you bench press them, you know? I mean they'd change the angle all the time, so we did work to do multi-angular type of training—running primarily, and wrestling. And Sepp was very good at promoting. He loved wrestling, real competitive wrestling, and both Vic and I, we liked that too. So we would get in and we would drill. We'd just go over and over and over various moves, you know. We'd sit out and re-sit out and switch. We'd do whole series of things, and then we would wrestle too, we'd competitively wrestle. Sepp was a great guy to keep us motivated to do that. We both liked him and respected him, so we did what he told us to do.

JS: And you still stay in pretty good shape. I mean, you told me you're a trainer still, like a personal coach.

DC: Yeah. I'm 77, but I still work out. But it's mainly lifting weights now. I don't do ... much. I was on the mat the other day with a martial artist.

JS: You'd written me that you got some guy. What was that hold that you got him with?

DC: Well, it was just a head and arm, basically. Something I'd used in the past, and I just took him down, and it was just instinctive. I've done it so many times. It's kind of a reflex. I had him in a reverse arm bar— the arm bar is such that there's tremendous ... I mean, you could break a guy's arm if you wanted to do it. I didn't break his arm, but I put it on hard enough so he knew [*chuckling*]. He was hollering.

JS: He was screaming?!

DC: Yeah, he really was. He was hollering. And then another guy, a yoga guy, he says, "What's a nelson?"

JS: Uh-oh [*laugh*].

DC: I mean, you know, a quarter nelson, a half nelson, a full nelson ... So I say, "Well I use a reverse nelson, and it's just a ..."

JS: That's from the front, right?

DC: Yeah, well, the reverse nelson is on the mat, actually. Or the one that I use is on the mat. Basically, you bar the guy's arm, and he's up on his side, and you got his forearm barred, and you just kind of use your weight. It's painful as hell. It's very uncomfortable. So he said, "Ow, ow, ow." I let him go, but some of those guys were pretty wimpy. The guys I worked with [*laughing*], wrestled with—none of those guys would've hollered at something that simple. They'd holler at some of the other joints, other kinds of stretches ... Why, we were pretty tough. We would suck it up, but ... [*chuckle*]. So those were some of the things that we did.

JS: And it sounds like you really favored the head and arm into the arm bar.

DC: I did, and there were other things I could do. I could do things with my feet and legs. I trained them so I could almost use them like my hands. For example, if you're on top of a guy in the down position on the mat, where you're on offense and he's in defense, I would sometimes just pull him so he would post his left arm, you know, plant his weight on his left arm, and then I would just use my right foot and sweep his arm back into an angle underneath my left knee on the mat, then I'd just sit on it. That meant that I had one arm trapped, and I didn't have to do anything, so I had other body parts free. I had more body parts free to attack him. It's hard to explain something like this on the phone. It'd just be easier to show a guy, you know.

JS: Yeah.

DC: So we'd do things like that. And that'd lead to, you know, where you got two arms against the other guy's one. His one arm is trapped. It's kinda like a double wristlock, where it's a two on one. This is a little different: you got two on one, and then I'd get a reverse nelson, or something like that, and pull the top of his head because that's where the best leverage is and try to put that under his right armpit, you know. So, some of these things were ... [*chuckle*] they sound awful, but you don't break anyone's bones that way. You stretch a guy's muscles, and if they're not used to having them stretched, why, they holler.

JS: Yeah, they think it's the end.

DC: Yes, exactly. So that's some of the things we did. As I say, you were asking about the head and arm. I liked that move. I also liked the single leg dive, but on that, I'd try to set it up. Maybe I'd move in one direction, and usually the wrestler will kind of slide and glide so that both feet are on the ground most of the time, and I'd try to catch him in mid-move. I'd move in a direction where he'd be moving with me, you know, try to get him to circle, and then, when I'd see his foot is just about to hit, I would reverse direction and hook his ankle. Then I'd just pick his ankle, and I can pull him in or take him down or leg drag him. There are different things you can do. So that was another one of the moves I'd do. I can't remember them all. Sometimes I'd work out, just like these martial arts guys. I just did things reflexively, you know ...

JS: Muscle memory, huh?

DC: Yeah, exactly, yeah. You just kind of . . . It's there. Why, Sepp drilled us on this so damn much that everything was just reflexive. I think I sent you some of the drills that we used. We'd do various maneuvers, you know, and we'd start doing those loosely and let the guy work, and then pretty soon we'd work tighter and tighter and tighter so that everything became kind of a reflex in the ring. I would just guess that Hodge and some of those guys probably did similar things, maybe naturally or maybe through training, I don't know.

JS: Yeah.

DC: I never had the opportunity to work out with Dan—I wish that I had—but you're one up on me [*laughs*]. He was one of the true amateur greats.

JS: Yeah, he's a real amazing character. He really just showed me some ideas in street clothes, no real workout.

DC: He was a hell of a boxer too. He's a great athlete, I think.

JS: A Golden Gloves champion.

DC: He's a nice man, you know.

JS: I met Dan, and we just traded thoughts on double wristlocks. He had a little different technique than I did, and we just, you know, showed each other the move, and that was about it. We were both in street clothes and just, kinda, [*chuckle*] sitting around eating lunch and stuff. We talked about it, and that was it. I haven't seen him for years.

There's [a] controversy within the catch-as-catch-can little sewing circle that maybe you can chime in on. There seemed to be a little competitiveness between Lou Thesz and Karl Gotch. Karl I think had wrestled in the Olympics for Belgium.

DC: He did, but he lost to a guy that I had worked out with, named Henry Wittenberg. To lose to Wittenberg is no big deal because Wittenberg was the best wrestler of that 1948 Olympiad that Gotch was in. If you were the champion of all of Belgium, it'd be like being the champion of the state of California. Nothing to sneeze at, but I think Gotch got tougher after he went to school over in Wigan and learned some of the hooks. One-hundred-and-eighty-pound (82-kg) Ben Sherman handled Gotch when he was over in Europe before Gotch knew anything about hooking.

JS: Right, and this was before he went to Billy Riley's gym.

DC: Yeah, exactly. So it does make a difference. If a guy is a hooker, he's got a chance with anyone because [*chuckling*] if you get a guy hooked, he's hooked, you know. So with Lou and Gotch, I don't know if they ever had a chance to figure out who was the superior wrestler. I think they both had some hooking knowledge. I don't know Karl at all. I've never met him, but I do know Lou. I never worked out with him is all. I tried to work out with him twice when he was in Seattle, but he didn't show up. So I don't know. The difference between the works then and the works now is [*chuckling*] that a lot of the guys that were working then could wrestle too, you know. That's basically the difference. But there's been works in wrestling for a long, long time. When I was working, though, it was a closely guarded secret, you know.

JS: Right, right. The whole kayfabe thing. ["Kayfabe" in the pro-wrestling business refers to the act of not letting those outside the business know that the outcomes were predetermined or "fake." The term supposedly comes from the secret language spoken by carnivals workers to keep their customers or "marks" in the dark about how their games worked. Some say the language is similar to Pig Latin and "kayfabe" is carny-speak for "fake" or "be fake."]

DC: Yeah. To get back to Lou, Lou could wrestle some. Very quick fellow, but I don't think he was the best wrestler during his time.

JS: I've actually heard that Ed Lewis had said [Lou Thesz] was athletic, he looked good and all that, but that "Hunky" wasn't that great of a wrestler, but he looked great though. That he was more on the performing side.

DC: Exactly. He was a great performer and looked like a great wrestler, but you're absolutely right. Don't get me wrong, Lou could wrestle some too. I mean, some guy off the street wasn't going to beat him, but he wasn't the best hooker or the best wrestler around. Lou told me one time that Ed Lewis beat him in less than a minute.

JS: That's really amazing, and that was probably when Lou was still a young man, fresh and full of life, and Lewis was probably older by that time.

DC: I think that guys like Dick Hutton or Dan Hodge would've beat him, you know.

JS: In a competitive way.

DC: Yeah, in a competitive match. Lou is by far the greater performer. There's no doubt about that.

JS: Yeah, when it came to a competition about a bigger gate, Lou was winner, hands down.

DC: Exactly, yeah. He'd win it on what was called green points. Dollar points [*chuckling*]. In a competitive match, why, I think Hodge or Hutton or any number . . . There were quite a number of guys, I think, who would beat Lou.

JS: It always was troubling to me that if somebody has not had a competitive career, a legitimate competitive career without works, without performances and whatnot, how could he be called a hooker, you know what I mean?

DC: Yes. Exactly. The At Shows was probably the only place where there were any legit matches for a lot of years, and there weren't many of those. As I mentioned earlier, why, the places where you'd get a real competitive match would be in logging towns or mining towns or somewhere where they had a couple of town toughs, you know. And a lot of times those guys weren't that . . . I mean, from the standpoint of a technical wrestler, they weren't that difficult to beat. They were just big, strong guys is all.

JS: Right, but they didn't know the proper leverage, or the whole . . .

DC: Right, exactly. You've probably worked out with guys that were probably pretty physical but didn't know much.

JS: To me, that's always the funnest kind of match because I'm a tall and lanky guy, so I'd love to grapple one of the big bodybuilder type guys. This was when the Ultimate Fighting Championships first came out, before grappling became real popular. I was in college at the time, and I'd work out with the guys at the school, and nobody knew submissions then. It was always just the amateur wrestling guys. I had such a great advantage back then [*laugh*] because nobody else knew the submissions.

DC: Right, exactly, yeah. And that's exactly the way it was when we'd go into a logging town. The guys wouldn't even have an amateur background. You know, their idea of wrestling was to grab your head and a lot of times a standing headlock. Well, that puts you behind them, but [*chuckling*] they're putting themselves in a bad situation.

JS: You've already got the go-behind.

DC: Exactly. You don't have to work for anything. You just give him your head, and he'll do all the work for you. The same with amateur wrestlers. Of course, they were familiar with some things, so you had to have a little different approach with them, but they were not familiar with front face lock, toeholds, various types of arm bars, and head cranks, you know. They couldn't do those because they violated the rules, in spirit of the amateur rules. So it gave you a heck of an advantage.

JS: Now, I'm very suspicious when I hear someone call themselves a hooker if they've never had a competitive background, you know what

I mean? In terms of trying to pawn it off like you are a legitimate submission guy.

DC: Right. It's like one of the guys I was talking to. There'll be guys that, maybe, know three or four hooks, but they don't know the flow. There's kind of a flow to wrestling, you know, where you'll do one thing, the other guy counters, and then you'd counter that, and there's a wrestling flow. And the guy might know two or three hooks, but when you get him down, he can't actually wrestle.

JS: Yeah, they can't chain it together or use their weight the right way.

DC: Yes. They just know this move and that. They know the moves in isolation. I don't know how to say it, but I've seen that in the gym. We used to have pro matches down in the basement of this gym. They had a mat. It was just a mat. It wasn't a ring. All the competitive wrestlers would go down there and work out. The workers wouldn't show up because they didn't want to get embarrassed, you know.

JS: Yes.

DC: Some of the guys that were on top were good. Great performers. Great, charismatic guys that, you know, could work the crowd well, but they couldn't wrestle. As Sepp used to say, "The man couldn't wrestle a lick." You know that was what the old-timers would say of the guys that were non-wrestlers. They'd say, "The man couldn't wrestle a lick."

JS: And he may have been the type that looked great, was muscular, had a good smile, and could put butts in the seats, but you get him in there, and he wouldn't know the difference between a single leg and a fireman's carry, or between an inside and an outside toehold.

DC: Right. Because they just didn't have the background. You know, there's a sort of wrestling that I find works best for me and best for most guys I know. Holds don't just happen. For example, Joe Stecher was a very good wrestling technician, but he couldn't beat Ed Lewis because Lewis was a very patient wrestler and very strong.

Also, there's stuff out there, Jake, that you don't see published in books. There was a guy named Bud Anderson, who had just an extensive knowledge of hooks. Bud was a little guy, about 150 pounds [68 kg], but wherever he could touch you, he could hurt you. He just had great leverage. Very good. I've seen him embarrass some big, big guys. He'd taught me quite a bit. He'd shown me a lot of stuff, but when I asked him about a particular move that he'd used, he wouldn't show it to me. I said, "Well, Bud, why would you not show me this?" He says, "You know too much now, Dick." He just did not want to be wrestling his own stuff when he wrestled me. I loved to work out with him [*chuckling*]. He was a tough guy, but I liked to work out with him because you learn, you know.

JS: But he wasn't about to give you the keys to the kingdom, either [*laughing*].

DC: Exactly. He showed me other stuff, but then there are some things that he'd say, "That's it, you know enough," you know. I got to the point where I was bigger than him, and he couldn't handle me primarily because of the size, but also because I knew a lot of his stuff. So it hampered him. He was a very good wrestler.

JS: And you said his name was Bud Anderson?

DC: His name was Bud Anderson. Little-known guy. One time, this one guy came to the gym . . . He was a world champion and wrestled under the name of Ali Baba. He was, I believe, an Armenian, really, but anyway, he'd come down to the gym, and little Sepp said, "Why don't you work out with little Buddy Anderson?" And Bud just stretched him. That guy was the world champion, heavyweight champion, you know, weighed about 220 [100 kg], I think, and [*chuckle*] Anderson weighed about 150 pounds [68 kg], and he just stretched this guy . . . This guy's screaming. But it was kind of a lesson for some of the other pros. Some of the performers quickly got out of there. Bud Anderson was a very capable wrestler. Bud had to be one of the greatest technicians that ever lived. Sepp was also a very good technician. Sepp would like to attack one part of your body and just kind of wear that body part down, whereas Anderson was very versatile. He could attack you anywhere, and he could hurt you from any angle that he could grab you. When you worked with him, you had to do some thinking, you know [*chuckle*]. With Sepp, why, you knew you were in for a long, grueling pull-and-tug type of match. With Anderson, why, you had to be aware of a lot of things because he could hurt you. One thing he showed me was called, at one time, the West Point Ride. And I think it came from, uh . . .

JS: Jenkins?

DC: Yes, Tom Jenkins. He taught it at West Point. It's a very, very tough move, and it's real easy to apply. It doesn't take a lot of strength, you just got to be able to reach around a guy's chest.

JS: It's from *par terre*, right? You're in referee's position on top, and then you reach under or something?

DC: Yeah, okay. You reach around his chest, I mean, you hook. Let's say, you're riding him on his left side, and one arm is around his waist, one arm on his arm. Well, you reach up with that arm that was around his waist and hook him around his chest, and you hook your own arm, which is right at about his triceps level or his biceps level. You got your left arm on his biceps, your right arm is around, and you just hook your own arm.

JS: Okay.

DC: And you jump to the other side and walk him diagonally—just walk around his head—and that thing will tighten. It's not actually you squeezing or anything else. It's just the twist that you put into it. And it's a terrible crimp, it really is. It's really painful. It feels like your scapula is being separated from the rest of your body.

JS: Interesting!

DC: It's a very simple and easy move, you know. It takes a little practice just to work it correctly. But that was just one of the moves that we did. The front face lock, of course, and the double wristlock. Those were pretty well known. Everyone has a little different version of the wristlock, and you just have to work with what's good with your biomechanics, you know. Some guys would grab the palm of a hand, and some guys would twist the wrist. People have different ways of doing it.

JS: Yeah, some people grab the fingers.

DC: Mm-hmm. I was going to mention one other thing that is little known. You won't see it. I don't think I've ever seen it published. A double-leg dive counter. Generally, if you double-leg dive a person, they'll sprawl. I mean, you know that's kind of a standard defense. I just kind of discovered it myself. I thought I had invented something, but then Bud Anderson said that move's been around for a long time. But, anyway, I found if a guy's sprawled, you just reach up and grab his buttocks. Pull the buttocks right into your chest. You can pick a guy up by his buttocks, and it's actually a really helpless feeling. So if you get a chance, try it sometime.

JS: Hmm!

DC: Leg dive the guy, have him sprawl, just reach up, get his buttocks, and suck him right in tight to you. You'll be able to pick him right up. [*laughing*] It's the easiest thing ever done.

JS: Hmm! Sort of like a high crotch lift.

DC: Yes. It's actually pretty easy, too. As I say, you just grab the butt, down fairly low, and you pull him in. You render his legs powerless. It's kind of an interesting thing. Try it in the gym sometime. You'll see what I'm saying.

JS: I will, I'll give it a spin.

DC: Yeah, there's all kinds of stuff like that I don't see . . . You know, I can't remember. When I get up and start rollin' around, I just kinda do it. I can't remember [*laugh*] ahead of time. It's hard for me to remember that stuff.

JS: Well, I don't want to waste any more of your time. I think you've been really generous. I appreciate it, sir. I'll talk to you very soon, and thank you so much for your time.

DC: Oh, you're very welcome.

★ ★ ★ BILLY WICKS (1932–) ★ ★ ★

BILLY WICKS (A.K.A. "POPS") is a Minnesota-born professional wrestler, a hook wrestler (with Dobson United Shows and United Carnival Shows between 1951 and 1956), and a retired law enforcement officer. He came up as a wrestler with Red Bastien, learning under their teacher Henry Kolln, who had been a student of Martin "Farmer" Burns.

JAKE SHANNON: Pops, thanks for talking with me like this.

BILLY WICKS: Good morning, Jake. I appreciate you taking the time to inquire about this. You've got to keep in mind, of course, that I am a dinosaur from another generation of wrestlers. I am not familiar with a lot of the MMA, mixed martial arts stuff, and all the words you use. I'm used to using the words "wrestling" or "grappling."

JS: How did you get involved in wrestling?

BW: I guess I started when I was about 15 years old, with the Ober Boys Club in St. Paul, Minnesota, down on Western Avenue. A fellow by the name of Mr. Davis showed me a takedown, a leg grab. I thought that quite impressive, so that's really how I got started. Like I said, I was about 15 years old.

When I was about 16 years old, I met a kid named Quentin Dale Clark and he taught wrestling at the YMCA in downtown St. Paul. He invited me down. He was like 21 or 22, and I was like 16. He was quite a well-built kid. He quite impressed us guys when he came up to us when we were hanging around the corner one night. What got me attracted to it was that he could handle me or anybody else at the beach at Phalen Park in St. Paul, Minnesota. He could handle us guys in front of all the girls. I guess that got to my ego. You know how us young men are.

JS: [*laughs*] Yes.

BW: Then, later on, after I learned how to wrestle, when I was about 19 years old, I ran into a professional lady wrestler. She was working at a department store, and she had a lot of bruises on her arm.

I said, "Boy, your boyfriend sure mistreats you." She said, "No, I am a professional lady wrestler." I was quite impressed with that. I said, "I wrestle too!" She said, "You ever think of wrestling pro?" I thought, "Oh my God no." Of course, at that time I was watching Red Bastien and Swede Oberg. Red Bastien was my hero. Anyway, she was telling me that the pro wrestlers worked out up above a bar, the Dutchman's Bar. It was on Roberts Street in St. Paul, Minnesota. She invited me down there, so I went down, and they worked out on Wednesday and Friday nights.

I met carny guys like "Crusher" Bob Massey; Gene Shredder, the local promoter; Marv Wasson, a wrestler; and my best friend, who was killed just recently, Billy Carlson. He won Mr. Minnesota for guys over 40, for guys over 50, and for guys over 60. He was Mr. Minnesota. He was a terrific guy. Of course, when I was there, Billy Carlson was in the ring, and this guy named Massey said, "Get in the ring with him Wicks, and wrestle him." So I got in there and took Billy down and pinned him like nothing. You know, I had an amateur background, and Billy was just a well-built kid. Anyway, that's how I got started.

JS: Very interesting. Someone on our Internet forum wanted to know what five basic skills every catch wrestling novice should try to develop.

BW: I don't believe I have five basic skills that every wrestler should know. Each wrestler has to develop skills on their own. There is wrestling, and then there are wrestling holds. You have to learn to wrestle before you can apply the holds.

You have three basic styles of wrestling: let's go out there and pin the other man; let's throw the other man, which is basically Greco-Roman; or let's submit the other man. So, amateur wrestling is the basic thing you need to know, as far as I am concerned. After you learn that, there are about a thousand holds out there. You only need to know about a dozen good holds. Know them really damn good. Zero in on your dozen good holds. You don't need to know a thousand holds. You're not a better wrestler because you know a lot of holds. It basically gets down to your mindset.

JS: What are your personal favorite wrestling holds and why?

BW: I zeroed in on neck cranks, wristlocks, and toeholds. Those are the only three areas I dealt with. Of course, there are so many variations of these holds: front face lock, rear face lock ...

JS: Who was Henry Kolln?

BW: Henry was my first legitimate teacher. He trained with Farmer Burns. He was one tough old man.

JS: Who are your all-time favorite legitimate wrestlers?

BW: Well, I guess I'd have to say Henry Kolln number one, my old carny teacher. He was 63 years old, and I was 19, and he was stretching my butt. He weighed about 150 pounds [68 kg]. Every once in a while he mentioned a guy named "Farmer." I had no idea what that implied. Farmer said this, Farmer said that. I came to realize later on that he worked out many times with Farmer Burns. Of course, I know you are familiar with him.

Other guys would be Tony Morelli, Bob Cummings, Swede Oberg, Doug Henderson, Charlie Carr, Joe Pazandak. I got on the mat with all these guys, except Bob Cummings. And, of course, Red Bastien. Red Bastien will fool you. A lot of guys don't know that Red was a hell of a wrestler. He worked the carnivals, and he had a lot of training under Henry Kolln.

JS: Red is a very nice man. I know him through the Cauliflower Alley Club. What was your single most rewarding experience as a law enforcement officer?

BW: I can't say that I had any one experience, Jake. It's just that I enjoyed being in a position where I could help people.

JS: What do you call your style of wrestling? Is there a principle, philosophy, or characteristic that sets it apart from any other?

BW: Well, I can just say that my style, if you have to use that word, my style is actually amateur wrestling and carny wrestling, mixed. Causing your opponent to feel discomfort and a lot of pain while you're wrestling, that's the carny style. In the process, you're looking for your submission holds. Henry used to say, "Always look for a better wrestler than you. You can't really learn a lot if you keep beating the same guy all the time. Try to find the toughest guy that's out there." That was my philosophy. I want to look for the toughest guy I could find. It's your mindset. If you want to beat somebody, you have to have a plan. It's like a football game. In wrestling, you have to keep moving and controlling in a relaxed state, then look for your submission hold, then you apply that hold—and I am just talking tournament stuff here—with the attitude that this guy just raped my mother and I want to hurt him.

JS: How has wrestling helped you in your law enforcement career?

BW: When I went into the sheriff's department back in 1960 and I was assigned to the Memphis Police Academy, I was told to teach "defensive tactics." I told them that I didn't teach "defensive tactics," I taught "mechanics and techniques and controls of arrest." I figured, as a police officer, you could be defensive for only so long before you have to get offensive. You couldn't be politically correct and teach offensive tactics, so I always told them "mechanics and techniques and controls of arrest." In my class, I told them if you have to hit anybody with your nightstick, your flashlight, your gun, or your fist, you're a frustrated cop and you don't need to be a cop. Of course, that was back in the 60s, 40-some years ago.

JS: For those wrestlers interested in learning more about your style of wrestling, are there wrestlers or coaches that you would recommend?

BW: I think Johnny Huskey is the best. No doubt about it. I've seen a lot of wrestlers. Now, you see, I was dormant for about 25 years until Johnny Huskey picked me up about five years ago on the Internet. He contacted me and got me back into wrestling. Of course, he knew pretty good wrestling, but I showed him quite a few things that he didn't know, that he was impressed with. That is how we got our relationship going. Johnny is superior in any phase of submission wrestling I've ever seen.

JS: What do you think about the role of physical conditioning in wrestling?

BW: You don't have to do a whole lot of conditioning in wrestling. You'll find out what your condition is when you wrestle. Learning how to relax is the big secret in wrestling.

JS: Can you speak of wrestling in the carnivals?

BW: Most of the carnival stuff was worked. We had to have what you called a "stick" out in the crowd. We had to have someone in case no one came forward to wrestle. If you didn't have anybody to start the show off with, you couldn't make money.

A lot of people misunderstand the terms "amateur" and "professional." "Amateur" just means you don't get paid for your wrestling, but most carny matches were works. Most of the guys blew up after a few minutes anyway. It was a great experience. Back then, in those days, in the 50s, you didn't have mixed martial arts.

JS: How important are wristlocks to your wrestling?

BW: The side double wristlock is the bread-and-butter hold that I was taught by the old-timers in the carnivals because it is two on one, two of your arms against one of your opponent's. That's my favorite hold.

JS: Of all the ways to grab your opponent for a side double wristlock, what is the best?

BW: There are three ways. You can grab the wrist, grab the palm of the hand (like shaking his hand), or grab the four fingers and the thumb. I'll tell you, don't grab the wrist. If the man can make a fist he can use his forearm muscles. If I grab in such a way that he can't make a fist, then I take away about 30 percent of his strength.

JS: And always work on the left arm . . .

BW: Unless you know the guy is a left-hander. But I was taught that most guys are right-handed, so go for the left side.

JS: What about neck locks? All the old-timers didn't go into hundreds and hundreds of different holds that some people say catch wrestling has.

BW: No, no, no, that's right. There are three holds you need to know to be a hook wrestler: neck cranks or headlocks, side double wristlocks, and toeholds. If you know those three holds and know them well, you should be able to take out anyone.

JS: How did you get into professional wrestling?

BW: Tony Stecher, Joe Stecher's brother in Minneapolis, Minnesota. Also, Red Bastien, the president of the Cauliflower Alley Club. He was the man that was my mentor. He helped me get into my first territory and my second territory. He got me into Portland, Oregon, in 1957, and into Houston, Texas. I have to give a lot of credit to Red Bastien. Of course, he's a lot older than me [*laughing*].

JS: [*laughs*] Yeah, right. What was it like for you, going from the amateur style and the carny style into the pro style?

BW: I was a little disappointed. Like you, I wanted to compete, I was a competitor. Then I found out you didn't have to compete. You just do your thing. I was a little disappointed. But you got to travel a lot.

JS: Thank you so much for all this great information, Billy.

BW: Thank you, Jake. Keep your head up and your elbows in. You just keep studying the stuff I gave you. I'll talk to you real soon!

★ ★ ★ FRANKIE CAIN ★ ★ ★

FRANKIE CAIN IS A FASCINATING figure in the history of professional wrestling. He was involved in wrestling early on, as you will read in this amazing interview, and he has seen tons. Cain did nearly everything there was to do in his era of wrestling. He plied his trade as a carnival wrestler and boxer, taking on all comers (wrestler-boxers were known as "combo-men"), he wrestled successfully as both a tag-team and singles performer, and he was known for being one of the best bookers in the history of the business. I've spent much time picking Frankie's brain.

JAKE SHANNON: . . . And I think most people are probably familiar with you from the work you did in the mid-'60s with Rocky Smith and Jimmy Dykes, the Infernos, and then later on with the Great Mephisto. My interest is in the legitimate catch-as-catch-can side, the old school stuff. Maybe you could tell me a little bit about your time in the carnivals, the Toe Hold Club, your boxing stuff, Waino Ketonen, that kind of thing.

FRANKIE CAIN: Well, when the Toe Hold Club was originated in Columbus, Ohio, we went down and started working out. I guess I was about 10. Treach Phillips—Treacherous Phillips, a friend of mine that later turned pro and worked for about 25 years—he was there. George Strickland, another guy that turned pro out of the club, was there. Leon Graham used to come up there and work out. He turned pro and wrestled for about 20 years. But I was about 10. A lot of guys came down that were from Sweden. They worked in the steel mills and they wrestled, not amateur style. Of course, we never wrestled amateur. We didn't know what the hell we were doing. We'd just get in there and just try to grab whatever was available.

Back in those days, you had guys like Ray Steele. Oh, God, there were so many. Frank Wolf, a great hooker that later taught Karl Gotch when Karl Gotch first came from England. From Germany, I guess, Karl went into England, and from England then he came to the United States. He learned a lot of wrestling in England, but the one to put the finishing touches to him—which he would tell you himself, if you were to talk to him today—was Frank Wolf, my old coach. He was the one that polished him up and showed him the hooking element of the business. Of course, he was already an accomplished wrestler. Frank Wolf, he was the epitome of a great wrestler. Al Haft, that was a promoter for about 40 years around Ohio—a German—was a good friend of Frank Wolf's. So Frank would come down and work out with us at the Toe Hold Club, and he would tell Al Haft about us.

Then we went up to Ohio State University. A guy came down from the newspaper and did a write-up on us. We were doing the hooking-style wrestling. We didn't know anything about amateur wrestling. As a matter of fact, we had never seen any amateur wrestling. He took us up to Ohio State University. I think Casey Fredericks was there, then. He was the coach. He invited us to work out with his wrestlers, but we had to do it amateur style, and this was unfamiliar to us. You couldn't bend against joints. They'd go for rides and take-downs. That's the way they'd jack up points. It looked so strange to us because we'd started so young.

These old Swedish guys, and some from Lithuania, would come in [to the Toe Hold Club]. Now, these weren't professional wrestlers. They didn't wrestle for money, but they did a professional style that they had learned in Europe. They would come in, get on the mat, and they were thrilled to have a place to work out. So they would teach us this hooking stuff, which later would become very valuable to us when we went on the carnival.

JS: And Frank Wolf, where did he learn the hooks?

FC: He learned in Germany.

JS: I see.

FC: And all the great Europeans—not all of them, but most of them—had started as amateurs, but then they learned his hooking method. So when we went up to Ohio State University, Ben Hayes, the newspaper-man that took us there, said, "Let them wrestle their style." Well, we started moving around the mat. We'd hook them standing up, and they would scream like hell.

JS: [*laughs*]

FC: They were a lot older than we were. We were still kids, 14, 15 years old then. I guess they were about 22, 23, something like that. College students. So, of course, Casey told us, "Oh, no, you can't do that. You can't do that style here."

Well, in the matches—we're talking about professional matches now—where we went, the guys would use this method, but they would do it in a working sense. And we knew right away that they were work-ing, but they would use this hook method. The people, even though they didn't know wrestling, would sense that you were in a dangerous position. You were hooked in a dangerous hold. Now your job was to work out of the thing.

Of course, the heels would heel out, and the baby faces would make some kind of a move to get out. If you hooked him with it again, he'd have another escape route. Then he'd have another escape route. This is what thrilled people.

So when television first hit, they needed a lot of action on TV. Guys couldn't go in there and lie around. But they weren't really lying around. If they had a hold on a guy, and the guy zipped out of the hold, well, people don't believe you'd really got that hold on him. So they would get a guy in a hold, and they'd use all the dramatics they could to work the crowd up. That's why Ed Lewis and others drew unreal money.

Frank took me up to an old hotel in Columbus called The Chittenden. Ed Lewis had contracted an eye disease called trachoma. He got it from a Turkish guy that he wrestled. Now, Ed was actually recognized as world champion all over, I mean, all through Europe, all over the world. He went to India, and he'd go to England and Germany. He was recognized as the legitimate champion.

JS: Yeah, he was a legit guy. He could really go.

FC: Right. And when he got that trachoma—I don't know if it was his first episode of it, but he was really in a bad shape, and I was just a kid. I forget how old I was, maybe 12, maybe 13—I doubt if I was that old, but somewhere around there, between 10 and 13. I'd go up there, to Ed, at the hotel, and he had this medicine. Somehow, the pharmaceutical people weren't allowed, or they couldn't mix this stuff up or something, because he would get it in the mail. I'd go downstairs and wait for it. Frank Wolf would come up there and see him, and I'd go up there every day. He told me Frank was one of the most underrated wrestlers in the world. He didn't go on the road much, and he rassled around there for Al Haft. But he didn't like the working element of it. He never really got with it as far as giving the great performance, but he was a great wrestler.

JS: I met Karl Gotch recently. He was telling me of a conversation that he and Ed Lewis had regarding [Lou] Thesz. The way Ed Lewis said it, according to Karl, [was] "Hunky looks really good, but he couldn't really, really wrestle. He was too impatient."

FC: Right. Ed's right in that respect. I don't know about being impatient. Lou was a friend of mine, a good friend of mine. As a matter of fact, when I was promoting wrestling years ago, in Mississippi, he'd come down there and work for me and stay with me, and we'd go down and work out on the mat. He was a good amateur.

Now, you can ask Karl about this Frank Wolf, and he'll tell you, he'll verify what I told you. Karl is a hell of a wrestler. Still is to this day, a very powerful wrestler. He wrestled pro for quite a few years. Is he still living in the southern part of Florida?

JS: He is.

FC: But assessing Lou's talent, Ed would be right in that measurement of it.

JS: Yeah. That was always interesting to me because it seemed like he got so much legitimacy—Lou did—from his association with Ed Lewis...

FC: Oh, yes.

JS: ...But it ends up that it was actually more guarded, in a way, by Ed Lewis.

FC: Oh, yeah. Definitely. I mean, that's common knowledge to us old-timers.

JS: Now, this is the other thing. In terms of the legitimate type of hook wrestling, it seems like the last real place where that was happening was probably the ad shows, like the carnivals.

FC: Yes. Now, a lot of people think that was low class, but that's not true because most of your great wrestlers were carnival wrestlers. You take Benny Sherman and Waino Ketonen and the middleweight—I'm trying to think of his name, now. Oh Christ, I can't think of it right now. But he was on the ad show when I first went out on the road.

JS: Well, I know both Billy Wicks and Dick Cardinal, too.

FC: Yes. Both of those guys were tremendous wrestlers, tremendous wrestlers, and they had wrestled on ad shows for a number of years.

JS: What was your experience like in doing the carnival fights?

FC: Well, see, I started as a boxer.

JS: Oh, okay.

FC: I had boxing when I started. We used to have street fights back when we were just kids. A friend of mine would organize these fights. This was a big produce center, where I was raised, vegetables and so on, and all kinds of big farms around there would bring their stuff in to sell. Those big platforms, those loading docks, were between buildings, and we'd fight or rassle up on those loading docks, and people would throw money to us.

Henry Kolln. That's the name of the guy [the middleweight whose name Frankie was trying to recollect earlier]. Now, Henry had worked out with Billy Wicks.

JS: Sure. Henry Kolln.

FC: Yes, a great wrestler.

JS: He was a student of Farmer Burns.

FC: Yes, that's right, and he was a tremendous wrestler. A lot of guys will say, "Well, I can't understand how a good middleweight could beat even a fair heavyweight," but that's not true. These middleweights would annihilate these heavyweights, so there were a lot of class wrestlers. Benny Sherman, I don't know if you've ever heard of him, but he was a great wrestler. A Jewish guy. And, of course, Frank Wolf had wrestled him, and Karl.

A lot of them, you see, used to have big shows, Jake, and these big shows would have these fair dates. You'd go out on the bally and challenge. Well, hell, there's a lot of tough guys, so they'd get challenged, and this is the way that they would draw. Then they'd get a mark out of the crowd, or even a friend of the guy, to referee because they wouldn't want their own referee up there, in case the guy submitted, and then he said, "I didn't give up." Then there'd be a riot. So, you had to be very careful on the carnival. You'd try to beat a guy without hurting him and without embarrassing him. You'd try to go for the pin, if you could. Some guys were so damned wiry. They had never rassled, but you didn't know what they were going to do. They were so unorthodox and in such good shape that a lot of them were hard to handle. You had to clamp down on them and make them submit because it was very hard to pin them.

And, of course, the time element was of importance. So, if you got a guy in there and you got a good tip from him—a tip means a good crowd—then you would try to take him to 10 minutes, and then you have him challenge you again. Then you'd bring the people back through, about an hour later, for another 50 cents. That doesn't sound like much money, but it was a lot of money in those days. We'd just have a ring set up and have the canvas walls up.

JS: So there wasn't much overhead.

FC: There wasn't much overhead most of the time. Occasionally, on the big fair dates, they had bleachers. And on the Cole Brothers Circus, of course, that was an added show. You'd go out to challenge, and this is where Waino Ketonen would go and knock those guys off. He'd go up there and challenge. Hell, they would threaten to close the show down. They'd give him $25 or $50 to leave, but he'd be back a couple of days later, challenging again. Well, they didn't want to deal with him, so they'd close the show down.

JS: Wow.

FC: Yeah. He weighed about 170, 175 [77–79 kg], maybe, and he was a holy terror.

JS: Sort of like a Fred Grubmeyer, maybe?

FC: Yes, exactly, exactly. Only one time have I seen him get knocked out. The guy was so pitiful looking, so skinny, that Waino didn't want to rassle him. He told the guy, "Get somebody else. Get Frankie or somebody else to rassle him." But the guy insisted on rassling Waino, and Waino said, "All right." He came out of the corner and started to lockup with the guy. And you'd try to have that understood, that they were goofing with him for the lockup—a collar elbow—a lockup, they used to call it, and the guy threw a right hand, hit him around the chin. Down he went. Knocked him out. And he was so embarrassed by that, but he had a glass jaw. No one knew it. One punch.

No one knows what makes a guy have a lethal punch. No one knows. You can't teach it. You can't acquire it through association. You're born with it. You can teach a fighter to get better momentum, putting his shoulder into a punch, but you can't make a puncher. Punchers are born. They're natural born, and no one knows why.

JS: You're almost of the ilk of Danny Hodge, insofar as you had both boxing and wrestling. [Danny Hodge was both a wrestler and a boxer.] Granted, it's a different day and age, but you probably follow some of this mixed martial arts stuff on TV.

FC: No. I see it once in a while, but most of it here is pay-per-view, and I don't subscribe to it.

JS: Yeah, I'm just curious what your thoughts would be on how those guys are going about things because, I think, when you were doing it, though, you couldn't box and wrestle at the same time, right?

FC: Oh, yeah, on the carnival, yeah.

JS: Really?

FC: Oh, yeah. I was what you'd call a "combination man."

JS: Oh, I see.

FC: As a matter of fact, when I was boxing, you could move a guy around by reaching your hand behind his elbow and turning him. I had a pretty good left hook. I would reach down under his right arm and grab him by the elbow so fast that no one could see it, and I would spin him, but as I spin him I hit him with that left hook.

JS: [laughs]

FC: But now, in sanction matches, you can't get away with it . . . And then I would drop my head down into their collarbone. That would immobilize their arm. I mean, that's a shocking thing. I don't know if you've ever had it done in wrestling. You use your head like a battering ram right into the collarbone, but you'd do it so fast. You can't do it with your forehead. You've got to do it with the top of your head. You'd be in as much pain as he would because it's bone against bone. If he's a hell of a fighter, you've got to get him out of there because, if you sacrifice that man's money that's running the show, as a fighter, hell, he'd fire you. And you'd be out in some damn wilderness, somewhere, a thousand miles away from home. So you'd go in, and, hell, you had to be a holy terror.

JS: You had plenty of incentive.

FC: Plenty of incentive. That's to have enough money to eat the next day [laughing].

JS: Now, wasn't there an Olympic wrestler as well by the name Ketonen?

FC: Now, there were two Ketonens. One was called Paavo.

JS: The Olympic guy?

FC: You know, when I met Paavo Ketonen, I fought for him. He was handling boxers.

JS: Oh, interesting, okay.

FC: But he was a wrestler. Now, I don't know if Paavo was an Olympic wrestler. I know he was a good wrestler.

JS: But Waino Ketonen was an American. Is that right?

FC: No, no. He was from one of those little Lithuanian countries. Finland, I think.

JS: Okay.

FC: I'm not sure, but I think he was Finnish. But he learned to wrestle in Wigan, in England.

JS: Because I was talking to Karl Gotch, and he mentioned Ketonen, and he said that, yeah, he was a Finn but that he had done something at the Olympics for wrestling.

FC: Well, he was a hell of a wrestler, and he may have.

JS: And he was a hooker, as well. He knew the hook wrestling.

FC: Oh, yeah, he was a hook wrestler, oh yeah. I don't know how many years ago it was. I was quite young. I was 16 when I met him. He tried to work house matches with promoters but just didn't get along with them because, as a pro, you've got to do jobs. And I don't know if he didn't want to do the job, or what, but he ended up wrestling on a carnival. After he left the show, I don't know if he went anywhere and worked house matches. If he did, I never heard of him. Of course, every state had its own territory, so he might have gone off somewhere, but I think he went back to England.

JS: I see. That's very interesting. I've tried to find information on him, and it's scarce.

FC: It's scarce, isn't it?

JS: Yeah.

FC: Yeah. I didn't know Karl Gotch knew him. But of course, the old carnival wrestlers I was with died. I never met anybody that knew him. As a matter of fact, when you mention them old carnival wrestlers, nobody really knows him, you know what I mean? When you mention Henry Kolln, you don't find him either, in the annals of history of great pro workers.

JS: Yeah, I've only heard of him from Red Bastien and Billy Wicks, and that was it.

FC: Yes. He was wonderful. Oh, my God, then there was another named Jack Sherry.

JS: I've heard of him.

FC: Yes, and he worked on the At Shows. He was a hell of a wrestler. Have you heard of Ben Sherman?

JS: Yeah. This was another character. I had heard the name, but again, it was Karl Gotch that said something about his changing his name? That his real name wasn't Ben Sherman? I couldn't remember, right off the top of my head, what he was saying, but he said he was a heck of a wrestler.

FC: Oh, yeah, I didn't even know he'd changed his name. Of course, I'm going way back, many, many years, and he was always Ben Sherman to me. I never knew him ever to have had another name. Now, he may have had because he might have gone into a territory where they had a Sherman, and they may have told him he had to change his name.

JS: That was the thing that Karl said, that he was actually an Irish and German guy, but he changed his name to sound more Jewish because of the territory he was wrestling in, or something, to make more money.

FC: Might have. Might have.

JS: Now, in terms of learning the old-style hook wrestling, I keep hearing that it's a lost art, really.

FC: Oh, yes.

JS: What is a young guy like me to do? How can you learn the old legit style? Because I've done a little bit of pro wrestling, the worked matches, some amateur wrestling, and submission grappling, but I'd like to learn, in a purist kind of way, the actual hook wrestling.

FC: I don't know of anybody. Now, there are probably some out there in California, but the ones that I knew, Jake, they would be too old to teach. Like me. I couldn't get up and down. I can teach from the side-lines, but you'd have to have one hooker in the ring to teach you.

JS: Yeah, to actually go through the motions and the moves.

FC: To go through the motion. And I couldn't go through the motion. Christ, I'm 78. And Jake, I don't know where in the world you'd learn it . . .

[Shooters] would use their knees, and they would use what you call "slide wrestling." Like a guy coming into a baseball mound, they would slide in. Wrestlers used to slide into you like that, then they'd go for the opposite leg. They'd hook your leg on the back of their knee, the bend of their knee. They would come in and grab your ankle, take your other foot, shove you down, pull on your ankle, shove on any part of your body. You're going to go down. And even without using their hands, they would be on your ankle and have you hooked on the back of their knee. Do you kind of understand?

JS: I can visualize . . .

FC: They'd use their body and press towards your foot. They'd like to tear your ankle out. So, I don't know who in the hell could . . .

Now, these guys you're telling me about, that are on TV, you'll notice, in these shoots I see on TV, they do a leg pickup or a double leg pickup. They do it all the time. Then the guy front face locks him, and then they lie there for a little bit. Why don't these guys ever go behind each other? That was what we were taught to do. To spin behind, go behind a guy, and then take him down. For what little bit of wrestling I see, I've never seen that move. It's just ironic. I never see it.

JS: Yeah, you rarely see them doing the go-behind.

FC: Yeah, you go so low when you do shoot to go behind them, but, these guys, sometimes they'll try to go behind, but they're damned near standing up.

JS: Right [*laughing*].

FC: So you're right. It is lost.

JS: Yeah, it's kind of frustrating because I'm just so interested in the history of it, and it seems very effective, very scientific.

FC: Oh God, yeah. I started in the working matches after Al Haft started using me, and I was only about 16 then. My ears were already cauliflowered, my nose had been broken from fighting, so I had that rugged appearance.

JS: Yeah.

FC: So he started using me. Then I had to get used to another style of rassling—the working, thrilling the people—or else you'd starve to death because no one paid to see a shoot.

JS: Right, because it's so boring.

FC: It's so boring.

JS: Now, you had a pretty good run. You were very successful with doing the worked stuff, too, later on, and you wrestled under the mask.

FC: Yes, for a lot of years. As the Inferno. As a matter of fact, that was my gimmick. I got the team together.

JS: Oh, really?

FC: Oh, yeah. Then when I came out from under the mask, I went as the Great Mephisto.

JS: Yeah, I was reading somewhere that it was a supernatural gimmick, or whatever.

FC: I was the first one ever to talk about, I would mention my opponent, but I would talk about auras that I've seen around different people . . .

JS: [laughing]

FC: . . . And then I'd drive the promoters nuts. I would tell them I could see the aura of self-loathing. This is why they'd become thieves. And I would really give it to them. They wouldn't know what the hell I was talking about.

JS: Now, is it true that even Anton LaVey [the famous Satanist] contacted you?

FC: Yes.

JS: What was that like? He was a character, huh?

FC: Oh God, yeah. I had never heard of him. I used to do a sign with my little finger and my thumb when I talked, and I'd copied it from Anton Leone. And I don't know why he did it, but when he did his interviews, he would do it like that. So I finally remembered that gesture, and I remember it got people's attention, but it's the Sign of the Ram, and I didn't know that.

JS: [laughing]

FC: That's how dumb I was. I didn't know what the hell it was.

JS: So Anton LaVey contacted you?

FC: Oh, yeah. I had that belt. I was out there for Roy Shire when we were drawing, Christ, $80,000 houses back in those days.

JS: Wow.

FC: Then I punched him out, and then they blackballed me from the business, but I was ready to quit. I was getting up [in] years, and I was ready to quit anyway, and I went in for—oh, the guy in Texas, what was his name—Paul Bosch. He used me, but the rest of them had me blackballed. That's when Eddy Graham and others were going to go out there and take Shire's territory because Shire was going to go along with them. The territory was in such bad shape. No one wanted to work for him because he was such a prick, and that was the last guy to draw all this big money. After I left, the territory went down and stayed down. When [Anton LaVey and his people] came to talk to me, they came in a big stretch limo and had some beautiful girls with them.

JS: Now, was this in San Francisco?

FC: No, it was in Sacramento, but San Francisco is where I went to his house. He had a big black house and a big black . . .

JS: I used to live in San Francisco, and that's the reason why this story, when I saw it, I was shocked because he was such a character. I had driven by the house. You actually went inside, huh?

FC: Oh, yeah. They took me in there. So LaVey thought that, with the name Mephisto—which means devil—and the Sign of the Ram that I was doing, I was a devil worshipper.

JS: So, whatever became of that? Like you hung out with him, obviously. He was quite a character, huh?

FC: Oh, no. I didn't, no. I just met him one time.

JS: Oh.

FC: What happened is I wrestled Peter Maivia, and a lot of Samoans jumped in the ring. Well, when they jumped in the ring, the cops handcuffed him. They had to call a riot squad out, and the Samoans that were handcuffed with their hands behind them, they ran off with the handcuffs on.

JS: [*laughing*]

FC: [*laughing*] So there were a lot of Samoans out back. We used to come out of the back door of the Cow Palace. They were out there. They were waiting for me. They were going to kill me.

JS: Oh my God!

FC: And LaVey's people, they'd come in, in this big stretch limo, right behind the door, and they had some beautiful girls there. So they asked me, "Can we talk to you?" I'm thinking, someone had kept telling me, "Now, Frank, these people are wealthy people. They want to start a shoe factory, and they want you to do some commercials for them." I'm under the impression, "Who in the hell are these people?" They come up when I'm on television. They always appeared in San Francisco, and when something is out of the normal—there's an eerie thing to it. But I thought, "Now, I've got to get to my car. All them goddamned, wild-ass Samoans are out there, waiting to kill me. Here's his car. I'm going to let these people take me wherever in the hell they want to, so they can get me out of there."

JS: Sure.

FC: "I'll come back later and get my car."

JS: And all the pretty girls, I'm sure, didn't hurt either.

FC: Well, that's what enticed me. So I got in, and they took me to meet LaVey. And LaVey said, "You evidently are one of us." Well, when I went into the house, the house had all those weird things, and it just didn't look right. But they were very nice to me. And I told them, "No, you've got the wrong guy. No, I don't believe in no devil." He said, "Oh. We just misunderstood. We just wanted to talk to you." And he thanked me for my time, and all that. They took me back, and everyone had cleared out. And I got my car. It was just the one meeting with him.

JS: Man, you've got one of the most interesting stories in wrestling. Not just the stardom and the money that you were able to make, but also being connected with the At Show and then the Toe Hold Club and all that. It's really great.

FC: Well, back in them days, Jake, a lot of guys started on the carnivals. As a matter of fact, Gorgeous George was on the carnival. Not with that gimmick. Just as George Wagner.

JS: Right.

FC: But there were a lot of guys. Baron Leone. I don't know if you've heard of him.

JS: I've heard of him.

FC: He was a carnival wrestler. And then the guys I've mentioned, Henry Kolln, Waino Ketonen, those guys were great wrestlers. How long Waino was on the carnival, I don't know. But after that guy knocked him out, he left. Once a weakness is discovered in you . . . Before a guy puts a hold on you, a good right cross could take care of a lot of shooters. Always remember I told you that. A lot of guys, if they can't take a punch, you knock them out. And to be a fighter on the carnival, they didn't want the fight to go the distance. They didn't want to go four rounds, and then someone's got to render a decision. If you're going to protect the man's money that owns the show, the decision is going to go against you, and there could be a damn riot in the Fair Board. The Fair Board was always against the athletic shows because a lot of riots would happen.

JS: Yeah, people get so riled up.

FC: Right. The guys would go out, traveling around the show, and would bet those farmers. Not only the farmers—in big cities—and it would add to the heat, when the guys had to pay off. Some wouldn't pay off.

Some say, "All right. You bet on the carny guy," and then he would bet him. I would beat him. After maybe some time, you'd drag him through the tip two or three times. If he's a good athlete, if he's a pretty tough guy and could look halfway presentable, then you can get maybe three shows out of him.

JS: Right.

FC: But you're working and he's shooting.

JS: Right. That's difficult.

FC: Oh, it's terrible. And I did it both as a fighter and as a wrestler. Then, sometimes, the guy'd come say, "I'll give you $50 if you let me go the four rounds, let me get the decision." Then the guy that owned the show would split it with you.

JS: Right [*laughing*].

FC: We used to sleep on the Jenny ride, the merry-go-round floor. Then, when we'd made pretty good money, then we could rent a room. But it was hard. Eating them old, greasy hot dogs and hamburgers and rasslin' four or five times a night. They were fighting a couple of times. It was really, really hard, but we didn't know. Hell, we were kids.

JS: Yeah.

FC: We didn't know. You'd just go along. And so I realized, "God, if I don't learn how to work, I'm going to be in a hell of a shape." I had to learn how to work. Jake, it was like beginning all over again, just learning to rassle.

JS: Yeah.

FC: Only to work. As you know, a lot of great wrestlers could never work. You had to be a natural. It would be like shooting, now. You can learn to shoot, but you can't learn to work because it goes with timing.

You're going to learn holds, and you're going to learn to sell and when to die, when to come back, and learn to register.

But that timing is so important. A lot of guys try working. They will do what you expect them to do, but they'll do it two minutes too late or two minutes too soon. It's like a comedian. Gets up and he tells a joke. Five other comedians get up, they tell the same joke, but only one of them's funny.

JS: Right, because of the delivery.

FC: The delivery. You're absolutely right. So the working element of it was so damned hard. I don't know how this is going to sound, but with me, it was easy.

JS: Well, you obviously were very successful with it.

FC: Yeah, yeah. It wasn't easy, Jake, because you had a lot to learn, but there were a lot of great workers back in those days. The element of working, how you could captivate them people, hell, it was like an opera.

JS: You could tell, if you were a legitimate wrestler, that it wasn't a real contest, but your average Joe, they still probably were in the dark, a little bit.

FC: You're absolutely right. When television first hit, and they used guys, basically a heavyweight, to come in, they used a lot of them that they couldn't rassle, couldn't work. And they had villains, but they'd boo the villains with affection.

JS: Right.

FC: We used to have killing heat. When I used to go down—there's so many places I could tell you about. My God. Riots. When I was a kid, they sent me down as a heel, down to West Virginia. Them coal miners would come out there. They'd still have that coal dust on their faces when they come to the match. You know what I mean? Wipe their face off and run down to the matches. That was their main source of entertainment. This was before television. And to get through them people, my God, they had knives and everything. But knives, hell, can happen in any big city, not just West Virginia. I'm not knocking West Virginia, but through Texas and anywhere down through Louisiana and Mississippi. Oh, God. Alabama. It was a fight for survival. You had to fight like hell to get back to the dressing room. Now, there has to be something wrong with a guy if he knows, "I'm going to go in the ring next week, and I'm going to top what I did last week and make him more angry." You know what I mean? You had to be mental.

JS: Yeah.

FC: When I look back at it now I think, "How in the hell could we have been so damned dumb?"

JS: Like a masochist or something, huh?

FC: Yeah.

JS: Well, you hear stories about—not so much anymore, of course, since McMahon, Jr. took things over, but back in the day—about wrestlers getting stabbed, and . . .

FC: Oh, I got stabbed so many times.

JS: I think Freddie Blassie had acid thrown on him or something?

FC: I don't know.

JS: You've been stabbed?

FC: Oh, yeah. I've been stabbed. Well, I was cut, a long ways, but it really wasn't a stab. But I've been stabbed probably eight times.

JS: Oh, geez.

FC: And cut.

JS: By fans, right? That think it's real, or whatever, and they're mad at you.

FC: Oh, yeah. Well, they want to kill you. You had that killin' heat. In Texas, when they took the Infernos there, they had to build a ramp—not to get us out of the ring, to get us in the ring.

JS: Wow.

FC: They'd try to kill us going in the ring. Oh, yeah, and they had a lot of Mexican baby faces there. Oh, hell, it was a . . . When I look back at it, I would rather go get a job, now, drive a taxicab, doing any damn thing . . .

JS: [laughing]

FC: You know what I mean? I don't know how in the hell I did it.

JS: That's funny. But your background in boxing and in doing the hook wrestling, it must have come in handy when it came to actual, real situations.

FC: Oh, God, did it ever, did it ever. The hook wrestling I did when I was a kid . . . Like I say, if you ever talk to Karl Gotch, he'll tell you about Frank Wolf. Now, Karl could wrestle. He learned to wrestle in Germany, and he learned to wrestle in England. Now, Frank was up in years when he worked with Karl. You know what I mean? He was really an old man, but he showed him a lot. Karl Gotch himself told me that. Yeah, he was a wonderful wrestler.

You know, you don't really realize what you've been through until you're an old man and you look back over the years because you're too busy running up and down the highways and continuing to do things. But when you get out of the business, it takes you a while to look back. And you think, "My God. I wish I had had my camera and took pictures of all the wonderful guys."

JS: Yeah.

FC: All the people that I met, like Jack Dempsey and Maxie Baer, well, all of them, they refereed wrestling matches.

JS: Yeah.

FC: And you look back, and you think you can tell people about them, but you don't have the pictures.

★ ★ ★ YOSHIAKI FUJIWARA (1949 –) ★ ★ ★

THE LEGENDARY KARL GOTCH calls him his best student. Wrestler, actor, and artist Yoshiaki Fujiwara was born on April 27, 1949, was the training partner of Satoru Sayama (Shooto founder), Nobuhiko Takada (Takada Dojo founder), Akira Maeda (Fighting Network RINGS founder) and Antonio Inoki (the professional wrestler who fought Muhammad Ali), and also trained with and assisted in the training of Minoru Suzuki, Masakatsu Funaki, Ken Shamrock, and many others. Fujiwara also had some success as an actor in Japan, often portraying gangster types.

JAKE SHANNON: What is your advice to the modern submission grappler that wants to be successful?

YOSHIAKI FUJIWARA: Believe in your own intelligence and never give up. It's like a samurai fighting spirit, which is close to never believe

84

in losing, not for one second. Never believe you can lose, never. Never believe, and then attack. Always think attack.

JS: Are there any fundamental skills that you feel most grapplers today lack and need to address?

YF: I think that modern wrestlers have advanced quite a bit over the years, but maybe modern wrestlers are too dependent on not just drugs, but even things like food supplements.

JS: When you are coaching, what kind of conditioning do you make your wrestlers do?

YF: I adjust the conditioning to each individual depending on their physique and attitude. Every individual has their own special training setup.

JS: What training advice would you give to experienced grapplers? How about novice grapplers?

YF: Like I said before, well, my advice for both novice and experienced grapplers is to never give up. And one more important thing is to find a very good coach.

JS: Will you ever produce another instructional besides your Submission Master series?

YF: No, I don't plan to produce another instructional series. One reason is because I'm not as young as I used to be, and, even if I did produce one now, probably nobody would really be interested in it.

JS: What do you think of the level of grappling in promotions like Pride and K-1?

YF: I don't really think about the levels because the rules are different. So, for example, the wrestlers in K-1 are training for K-1 rules. The wrestlers for Pride are wrestling for Pride rules. So I don't think of the level.

JS: Do you like any contemporary fighters?

YF: Recently, I haven't been really keeping up with the contemporary fighters, so I don't know. I don't have any special likes or dislikes.

JS: We share a good friend and his name is Karl Gotch. He always mentions your name when I ask him who his best student was. Can you tell me your impression of Mr. Gotch?

YF: Oh, Mr. Gotch is a very good friend, and, more than that, he is my best teacher.

JS: Do you have any good stories to tell my readers about Kamisama?

YF: [*laughing*] Yes sir, I do have something very interesting. One time during training, Mr. Gotch got a very bad toothache. His toothache was interfering with his training, so he went to the hospital, or maybe dentist, and asked them to pull all his teeth out. They said it's dangerous. He said, "That's okay. Pull all my teeth out," and he went back to training next day with no teeth because he figured if he had no teeth he's not going to have any toothaches getting in the way of his training. He's so crazy, but I love him.

JS: When did you start training in wrestling? What were your first years of training like? Who did you study under before Mr. Gotch?

YF: I started training when I was 16. I bought a book, and I taught myself, and those first few years were really wonderful. I did a lot of weight training. I built my body up to get powerful. [*Shows a framed black-and-white photo of a wrestler.*]

JS: So, who's he?

YF: He's Kaneko. Kakeo Kaneko. Mr. Kaneko was also in a group with Rikidozan and some other wrestlers that were most popular at that time. Mr. Kaneko was my coach.

JS: What are your future plans (which organizations would you like to work with in the future, other career plans, etc.)?

YF: What I'd like to do is live in the mountains and make my pottery. Another thing, which I've already started to do, is sell special foods, like sake. Now I have a sake which is being sold all over Japan. The illustration on the label, I did that myself. And I'd like to travel all over the world and meet beautiful women and have good food [*laughing*]. That's a joke.

JS: How is your approach and strategy different for a shoot match versus an exhibition match?

YF: In an exhibition match, my object is to show my strength. In a shoot match, my object is to damage the opponent so he can never fight again.

JS: How would you respond to a street self-defense confrontation versus a competitive confrontation in the ring? What would be the major differences?

YF: The biggest difference is, in a street fight, you can run away, you can escape.

JS: What is your opinion of other styles, like Brazilian jujitsu, judo, sambo? What makes the style you learned from Mr. Gotch different from the other styles you know?

YF: The difference between the three wrestling styles you just mentioned is just the rules. And the next part of the question, my style is originally from Mr. Gotch, and after Mr. Gotch, everything became my own style, where I added my own things.

JS: In your opinion, what submission holds are the strongest and most likely to succeed?

YF: I don't think there's any superior hold. I think it's just like a lottery, where you just, you know, choose from many. And a lot depends on the situation and the opponent—what hold is going to be best—so, I don't have one that I think is the strongest.

JS: Can you tell us about your artistic endeavors, too? How did you discover your love of pottery and painting? Who are your favorite artists?

YF: I was always interested in sketching and painting, from when I was a teenager. And I was also interested in doing things with modeling clay and stuff like that. About 13 years ago, a friend of mine introduced me to the art of pottery making, and I've been doing it ever since. It's my love.

JS: Can you tell your history in acting? How did you make the transition from wrestling to acting?

YF: Fifteen years ago, or earlier, when I was still wrestling, I was on some TV program, and some people said I was very interesting, so I got more and more acting parts and some other things.

JS: Who is Kiki Bragard, and what role has she played in your life?

YF: Kiki was first on my staff as a wrestler, and then, when I moved to an office, she helped me organize it and get everything together with the office, and, on top of that, she's given me advice about many things, especially to do with foreigners.

JS: Of all your students and people you've helped train, who do you think was the most technically gifted?

YF: All the wrestlers I know, they all have their good points and bad points, so it's very difficult for me to choose one as the best.

JS: What is your opinion in general of Sayama, Maeda, Choshu, Takada, and Inoki?

YF: Sayama has good speed. I think Mr. Maeda is very agile. The technique he got from his amateur wrestling is very good, and he's very powerful. Takada doesn't have any special, noticeable techniques that stand out, but he's very balanced. The techniques he has and his strength and everything is very balanced. And Inoki, he has a lot of guts, real guts.

JS: What do you think of Shoichi Funaki's success in the WWE, away from his roots in shooting?

YF: There are many different roads we can take as wrestlers, and when he went into the WWE and became successful, he made me very, very happy.

JS: Are you currently training anyone in grappling?

YF: Well, actually, I have an American pit bull and a cat that I found, and I'm training them in grappling [*laughs*].

JS: Do you watch MMA and, if so, what was your favorite match?

YF: I know what S&M is, but I don't know what MMA is [*laughs*].

JS: Do you ever talk to Billy Robinson anymore?

YF: I've only met Billy Robinson twice. One time was at his gym when he was coaching, and then, another time, we were invited as guests to a wrestling match, wrestling show. But I haven't seen him since then. I haven't met him since then.

JS: What do you think of the success of Kazushi Sakuraba, Kazuyuki Fujita, and a number of Japanese pro wrestlers in MMA, with respect to how it affects the wrestling industry?

YF: I know of both of those wrestlers, but I've never met them. I haven't really met them, except we just greet each other when we see each other, so we've never really talked. But they really do their best, so that makes me happy.

JS: Thank you so much for your time, Kumicho.

YF: Thank you, Jake!

★ ★ ★ GENE LEBELL (1932–) ★ ★ ★

AUTHOR, ACTOR, JUDO CHAMPION and "Godfather of Grappling" Gene LeBell has taught grappling skills to several well-known wrestlers and authored more than a dozen books on grappling and martial arts. Born in California on October 9, 1932, he has won many championships, including the National AAU Heavyweight Judo Championship and the USA Overall Judo Championship, which he won back to back in 1954. He then became a professional wrestler. It made sense since his mother, Elaine Eaton, owned and operated the Olympic Auditorium in Los Angeles, which was one of the main pro wrestling venues in Southern California. He picked the brains of the pros about catch-as-catch-can and absorbed everything he could. Nearly a decade later, on December 2, 1963, in Salt Lake City, Utah, Gene would face off against Milo Savage in the first mixed martial arts match of the modern age. Savage was a light heavyweight boxer and was ranked number five in the world at the time. Gene choked him unconscious in the fourth round.

Gene is a pivotal character who has helped catch-as-catch-can transition back to a legitimate competition sport after it nearly died out during the heyday of performance wrestling.

JAKE SHANNON: Well, I have your grappling work, *The Encyclopedia of Finishing Holds*. I'll be damned if I find one hold in the old-timers' books that you haven't covered. You've got everything in that encyclopedia.

GENE LEBELL: Yes. In a lot of them, they use different names. The old-timers, when I first started in '07, which is 104 years ago, we used to call it foot and leg control. Now, 25 years ago, the Brazilians invented it, and they called it "the guard."

JS: [*laughs*]

GL: So I go to the Brazilians. They said, "We invented the guard," and I said, "You're full of shit." First of all, what it's supposed to be is "foot and leg control." You control the guy with the feet. You control him to roll him over and do whatever you want to do. You can move him away, kick him away, or whatever. They say it's the guard. A guy's demonstrating that to me, and he said, "Well, you've got to scissor him." I said, "If a guy can do a scissor on me, he's in trouble." It's the easiest thing in the world to hook a leg.

JS: Yeah.

GL: His legs aren't going to jump away.

JS: Yeah, he's sticking it right there.

GL: He's getting in a triangle for any of the practical moves. For something as simple as an arm bar, you've got to have your legs unhooked, so you can roll a guy over in a simple half Boston or full Boston crab.

Give him a wrack on the gut or the groin area, and over he goes. Just depends on your attitude, of course.

JS: I've seen the tapes that you did with Mando Guerrero, too. Those are great.

GL: The wrestler. He is a good wrestler, yeah.

JS: Now, did you work with him, with the hooks, as well?

GL: I did a lot of hooks. That tape was done about 15 years ago, so I think we only had one heel hook in it and not as many arm bars or neck locks as I would like to do. You take *The Encyclopedia*. I've got about 70 holds that we were going to put in that we didn't get in. You just can't put everything in. And I do things with a flair of comedy.

JS: Yeah, right.

GL: They either gotta love you or hate you.

JS: I love your facial expressions.

GL: The face of a heel. And in that thing I come off as a heel, sarcastic and everything. And built it up. Everybody wants to beat the hell out of me, and, at the end, they all come up wearing my T-shirt.

JS: Yeah, "I stole a shirt from Gene LeBell."

GL: Yeah.

JS: You know what? I met you last year at the Cauliflower Alley Club. When you wrote that letter to me, and you mentioned how, with you and Bob, how you'd gone through the whole thing in trying to retain your rights and people ripping your stuff off and things of that nature. It reminded me that, a year before, I think it was in the December 2003 *Black Belt* magazine, there was some guy who had ripped off your three-finger grip.

GL: The three-finger grip?

JS: Yeah. In that *Black Belt* magazine, and I remember you telling me about that. You were like, "Yeah, that guy, he stole my grip."

GL: Yes, he did. I invented that grip, and I'll tell you how. You find it before 1936, and I'll buy you a new hat. I was working out of the LA Athletic Club with about six pro wrestlers. Shooters, all shooters, and this guy, Ed Lewis, he just retired from pro wrestling, and they're doing shooting holds. He shows me how to grab four fingers around the blade side of your hand. Well, he said, "Do it on me," and my fingers weren't long enough, so my thumb went on the inside, between his fingers. And he said, "That's interesting," and he went on to tease me, and he did it to himself. He said, "You know, more of my fingers go around the side." He stopped the class. "Let's try this grip," he said, because you have the Greco-Roman grips and the freestyle grips. "Let's try this, Gene's three-fingered grip." You really squeeze your fingers together. When you do it, your trigger finger and your thumb, if you squeeze them real tight, you lock your thumb in. Are you familiar with it?

JS: Yeah, sure, I can understand that.

GL: Well, do it to yourself. Squeeze your thumb and your trigger finger and the long finger, and just squeeze it all together, and lock that thumb in.

JS: Yeah, it's like the knuckle of your thumb locks up.

GL: That's it, and your hand doesn't slip out as easily. So when I worked out there—my mother made me go there every Saturday, just to get rid of me—they said, "Okay, we're doing Gene's three-fingered grip." Now, since then, people have copied that. In *Black Belt* magazine and a couple of other magazines, they did a couple of fighting holds, different fighting holds, and there's a couple of variations of holds that I do. One of them is an arm crank. One of the master Brazilian jujitsu guys put it in the book and its cover. CFW published a book of a bunch of good grapplers. This guy is good and everything, but he put the wrong foot over to hook the guy. He puts his foot over his head, and the guy can spin out of it.

JS: [*laughing*]

GL: He puts it over his back, and he can spin out the other way. So I told the publisher, "This guy's full of crap. I want to see him," and I told him to tease the guy on it. Of course, I'm doing this tongue in cheek, not trying to be conceited. I just say, "Hey, you do it this way. That way's great, but if you do it your way, the guy can just spin out, arch and roll, or whatever, and he's behind your butt." So, a lot of people have copied different things I've done, and they do it slightly off, which is wrong. I make sure if I copy something that Jake the Rake does . . .

JS: [*laughs*]

GL: . . . I not only give him screen credits, but if I don't have it right, I'll say, "Hey, Jake, show me how you rake his eyes again."

JS: So let me ask you this. I think it was the 1954 Amateur Athletic Union Nationals that you won for judo, or was it . . .

GL: Yeah.

JS: Did you win '54 and '55?

GL: Yeah.

JS: And you had been working out with these old-timers, too, so . . .

GL: Oh, yeah. In fact, in '54 I won but I had a tough time. All these guys gave me a real rough time. I have it on tape—they did a little old eight-millimeter type—how I beat this one guy, who was very, very, very good. He was a lot better than me, but I think he sort of ran out of gas, and I got him down in a side ten and a scarf hold, and I held on tight. After about 10 seconds he gives up. So they give me the match, and I said, "Wow. Boy, I really hold him tight." Of course, I don't realize until a few years later, working with the pros: don't forget, when you pin his shoulders to the ground, lean that head back. I was thinking, "Well, you crush the ribs." It isn't that. You're cranking the neck.

JS: Yeah, yeah, I see what you're saying.

GL: So not only was I cutting his wind, but he gave up because of a neck lock, which was illegal. So the referee didn't know it, the judge didn't know it, and I didn't know it. So you've got four dumb people there. It gave me a hell of an advantage. The following year, I had a new training method. Training with a tire, a motorcycle tire, and gloves on. Pulling it and throwing it backwards, the opposite way a discus would be thrown, the opposite of doing pushups. It's like groin. And my techniques of getting in and throwing the guy were so much better than some of these same guys that were really good. I threw fairly handily.

JS: Just in one year's time.

GL: Yeah, well, of course, I'm working out eight hours a day, every day. Fanatic's fanatic. But the harder you work, the luckier you get. Karl, one day in the dressing room, showed me a downward arm crank with a wristlock. Well, he showed me that move, and it's been a thing that I've hooked a lot of guys with over the years. One of my kids that entered the Get Tough contest, the first one he did, he went in as a real tough guy, and he hooked the downward arm crank, he locked it, and threw him around in judo throws . . .

JS: Oh, was that at the UFC?

GL: Yeah.

JS: I saw that. Yeah, it was like a double wristlock.

GL: Yeah. So he became pretty good at it and threw the guys around and hooked them. I've got it on tape. It's always good if somebody does something and does it right, and not just get a lucky kick or a lucky something or other, if you're going for it.

JS: Now, did you ever think that grappling would ever get back to the level of popularity that it is today?

GL: I box. I grew up in boxing gyms, and I really believe in learning boxing. Learn to bob, weave, and stuff like that, and throw punches. I stole this from Ed when I was a kid. I was seven years old. He said, "You want to do Greco-Roman?"

And I thought "Well, that's too foreign for me to learn."

"You want to roll?"

I said, "Well, that sounds like something to eat."

"Do you want to do freestyle? Do you want to fight?"

Well, I figured, well, boxing.

"Or do you want to grapple?"

And I said, "Well, what's grappling?"

He said, "That's a combination of everything."

I said, "I want to learn that."

See, the way he worked, they just shot. There's no work in there, the way he worked out. He'd do anything. He'd slap the face and go into a wristlock. He'd knee you in the groin and then go into [a] half Boston crab. That was all part of it. A lot of laying the elbows right on the pubic hair. The guy folds over, gives you your leg, and you hook it. So that's sort of what I took to. You meet a karate guy, and they're all doing the stand-up thing. And you get Mean Joe Green or Howie Long in there, and they don't know any grappling or fighting. They tackle the guy. He ain't going to stop them. Down he'll go, and it's the best wrestler, right?

JS: Right.

GL: But now the boxers and the karate guys are learning grappling, and a few of the grapplers are getting knocked out by a left hook, so they're learning boxing. So the tough guys do a little bit of everything.

JS: Your fight with Savage, that was, like, the first mixed martial arts bout.

GL: It was the first televised, of the modern, the others weren't televised.

JS: I know guys, like—Tom Jenkins fought Tom Sharkey and guys like that. James Corbett wrestled with Farmer Burns, I think.

GL: Yeah, and a lot of those were worked. I know Dempsey wrestled a few guys, and some of the pros would put him over. Then he'd go against a guy, and he'd hook him—a good one, a main eventer that could wrestle—and they did that on different tours.

JS: Now, do you think that your early boxing training gave you an advantage?

GL: Oh, no doubt about it, no doubt about it. I put it in, a little bit, with the wrestling. The old wrestlers, they say, "Okay, let's lock horns." Well, sometimes you bob and weave from boxing, and, all of a sudden, you're behind the guy.

JS: Right.

GL: Everything complements each other. But a guy named Bruce Lee used to train with me, and he said, "Gene, wrestling will never be big because they want to see *Ha Ye*." In Hong Kong, he was a big star. I wish he would have lived another 25 years so he could see that the biggest commercial thing on television is pro wrestling. Of course, people change, and you've got to change with them if you're going to be in the financial venue. Lou says anybody that didn't work close, he beat the shit out of. I stood there a bunch of times and saw him wrestle guys and hook on them and ride them. He said, "I don't take a fall for you then you show off to the crowd, flexing," he said. "You're going to die." And he backed up everything. A lot of people didn't like him because he was so much for pro wrestling, finishing holds, that a lot of people just didn't care, but he told me that Karl was the best.

JS: Karl Gotch?

GL: Yeah.

JS: Yeah.

GL: But I saw Lou, and I was in Omaha, Nebraska, and I saw him work with a bunch of amateur wrestling champions, national champions, and just play with them.

JS: Do you think somebody of Karl or Lou's ability would fare well in today's mixed martial arts?

GL: Well, there isn't a guy that I would, in my prime, be afraid to go against. Karl and Lou were the most likely to stretch me. I mean, when I was in good shape . . . and I worked out every day.

We were in, I guess it was Omaha, Nebraska, and there were a couple of guys that supposedly were national champions, state champions, Oklahoma, and I went and worked out with this one heavyweight guy that was supposed to be the NCAA champion. I went about nine minutes—and he's strong as can be, and he weighed a hell of a lot more than me—and I finally got him down and hooked him. And then Lou was working out with these guys, and he's meeting them, really, like, playing with them. You just get very casual. And then, he said, "Okay," to this big guy, and I said, "He's going to have one hell of a rough time. How is he going to get him?" I mean, this guy's big and he's strong. He had me in the air a bunch of times, not finishing, but he's got me up there.

And, he picked Lou up, threw him down, and the next thing I knew—this is all in about a minute—Lou had him in an ankle lock, and the guy is screaming for help.

JS: [*laughs*]

GL: And I said, "Oh, fuck." And he got up slowly and was limping off, and he said, "That's great, but it's illegal." What are you going to say? Of course, it's illegal, but you don't play a guy at his own game.

JS: Right, right.

GL: If I'm going against a champion wrestler, he better be able to block overhand right. If he's a champion boxer, you tackle him, go behind, and grab a leg, an ankle. It's a long way from the heart. It's just horses for courses.

JS: You also were the referee for the Muhammed Ali and Inoki fight?

GL: Yeah.

JS: Wasn't Karl Gotch in Inoki's corner?

GL: Yes.

GL: I worked out with Inoki when he was in Little Tokyo, though he wasn't a great wrestler, he was a good wrestler.

JS: Why was he always kicking at his legs?

GL: Well, what Inoki did is, he trained with these wrestlers. He got hold of some Japanese karate guy who said, "If you kick him in the thigh, he'll go down." And so the guy kicked Inoki while they were talking, and it hurt, and he said, "Okay, you lay on your back, and you kick him, and then, he can't hit you while you're down." It's about the worst coaching as you could ever get, and Karl said, "Take him to tackle him, take him down and break his leg or his arm or his neck." He just did it his own way. I was told after it. Freddie Blassie said—he was there also—they were talking [about] letting Muhammed Ali or Cassius Clay beat up Inoki and then do a blade job—you know, a blade job—and I guess . . .

JS: Like cut himself, you mean?

GL: Yeah. Do it in the corner or something like that, but they didn't want to tell me because they wanted me to be like I'm in on it or something like that. I wasn't privy to this. I didn't hear it. I didn't talk to Clay about it, didn't talk to Inoki about it, but it was mentioned, and I guess Clay wouldn't go for it—make it look like he was beating the guy then he got a cut. So he said, "I can beat any wrestler anyway." I went to Clay's room, and he's looking at the pro wrestlers—I mean working them, and how he's going to beat them, and I said, "Oh, fuck, these guys aren't wrestlers."

So, anyway, it was a boring fight. Then, in the 15th round, Ali hit Inoki a couple of times, and Inoki said, "I wish I knew. He didn't hurt me," but they both weigh like 225 [102 kg]. That's a hell of a lot of weight. And you shouldn't get knocked down the first punch, but you don't take a punch like that. You don't have to. I mean, the guy can't grab you once he's down with gloves on. The gloves, nowadays, you put your fingers through. You've got a certain amount of grip. Not the greatest grip in the world, but you can't grab with eight-ounce gloves. So we put in the scorecard, and my score came out even. I didn't even keep track of it. And the wrestling coach voted for the boxer, and the boxing coach voted for the wrestler, so it was a draw.

JS: [laughs]

GL: And Ali went to the hospital for a few days with a blood clot on the left knee.

JS: Oh, geez.

GL: Above the left knee.

JS: So he did do some significant damage then.

GL: Yeah, but I wanted to bitch slap him. I thought, about the third round, I'd like to wrestle one guy and then the other guy . . .

JS: [laughs]

GL: . . . And take home the money. Ali got $6 million, Inoki got $2 million . . .

JS: Geez.

GL: . . . And poor Gene got $5,000. It was big money then.

JS: You wrestled under a mask as the Hangman for a while.

GL: Sometimes I wrestled under the mask, and I had an outfit they made in Mexico, in Texas, and a mask, and I said, "Jesus, it looks like you can see part of the face. I can see right through this." So this guy from Mexico puts an eye in the middle. You'd wrestle in some of the small towns, and then you'd come back and wrestle as another character with a different gimmick. And I was Henry, the One-Eyed Batman, and then I'd come back, and Gene LeBell was the asshole, with different styles.

JS: [*laughing*] Sure, and back then it was relatively dangerous, wasn't it, especially to be a heel, because the fans would actually come after you sometimes?

GL: My first week in Amarillo I got cut five times by fans. Of course, I got on television and said, "One Californian can beat any 10 Texans," but what really got me over is the first match I had. I was out of the ring, and they had a black section. This is funny. They had to go way up on the top, and this little gal, she must have been about five years old, cuter than a buck's ear, little black gal, and she had her pigtails with ribbons ...

JS: Okay.

GL: ... She came up and wanted my autograph. I picked her up and gave her a big hug and a kiss on the cheek and wrote an autograph. I'm picking her up and waving her to the crowd, and they were booing. I said, "Jesus. What did I do?" And she went back. It seems they're very, very prejudiced. Then I walk down to the dressing room. Past the dressing room, it says "Colored Drinking Fountains" and "Colored Bathrooms."

JS: Oh, wow.

GL: I didn't know they were separated. So when I get on television, the announcer said, "Hey, you went and gave a pickaninny, whatever they call them, an autograph. And I grabbed the guy. I don't know if he's working or shooting with me, and I grab him, and I said, "Look, my mammy is black."

JS: [*laughs*]

GL: And I shove him up against the side there. I'm working, but he's scared. He thinks I'm a psycho.

JS: [*laughs*]

GL: The next week the place is sold out. Then I did a gimmick that I'd take challenges out of the audience. If they could beat me they'd get $100, and, of course, they'd have to be born in Texas. So a guy would come up. Doc Sarpolis would put a cardboard box in the ring. We'd sit down, and I'd say, "I saw this guy in Chicago. He's not from Texas." Of course, he'd have a cowboy hat on, a 10-gallon hat and boots to match. Of course he was from Texas. "You've got to come back next week with 10 witnesses." Of course, all the 10 witnesses came back. Had to pay. No Annie Oakleys. And he'd come back next week, some big farm guy, so you'd take him down and have fun with him and then put him to sleep. And then Dory Funk, Sr., or one of those guys, would jump in the ring to save the day, and they'd beat the shit out of me and body slam me and everything. I'd get on television and say they were cheating and everything. But I'd take anybody from the audience, and we went for 16 weeks straight, and the houses kept on getting bigger and bigger.

JS: Wow. So it's almost like the old carnival wrestling gimmick, huh?

GL: Yeah, oh sure. That's it right there. The stranger-in-the-town type thing, sure, the same thing. But we had a lot of suits back then, in the '50s.

JS: Do you think things would be different nowadays? There's so many different videos out there, and everybody knows different little things about grappling, here and there. Do you think it would be a lot harder to run that kind of gimmick?

GL: That's a hard question to answer. It depends what you mean, "harder." For example, the grappling and the Get Tough contests are very popular. They're getting popular in Japan. But you get an audience of 1,000 to watch a grappling show, where they're shooting, or to watch a couple of pro wrestlers getting married in the ring or hitting on somebody else's wife in the ring. They're going to look at the soap opera, and so, it's what sells.

And I remember Lou—if a guy wrestled in the ring and tried to make a clown out of Lou, Lou would hurt him—and he used to wrestle this guy, Charlie Moto, Mr. Moto. And Charlie said to me, "I hate to wrestle Lou because I've got to throw salt to the four winds of purified air. He just beats the shit out of me. But," he said, "I make lots of money."

JS: [*laughs*]

GL: I was refereeing Karl—I don't know if he'd remember this—and I said, "Karl, I want to see a backdrop. I want to see this." I'm a referee, and I'm calling these things, and he's beating the living shit out of this guy, and I said, "Oh, *that* was luck. Do it again because I want to learn!"

JS: During a live match?

GL: He did it again.

JS: That's hilarious.

GL: The other guy is 6'6" [2 m], and about 270 or 280 [122–127 kg].

JS: Wow.

GL: In judo he won a lot from standing throws. His matwork was good, but not great. I could beat him on the mat, no trouble, but I couldn't have thrown him around like Karl did.

JS: Now, you've also had quite a few famous students from Bruce Lee and Chuck Norris coming in and doing some grappling with you. But

I don't think a lot of people know that Rowdy Roddy Piper is a black belt in your system. Is that right?

GL: Well, he's not braggadocious [*sic*]. You have to be, I think. I think he was 16. He used to come down to the gym and then work out really hard for a long time. He got damned good. I wrestled him a bunch of times pro. Then he eats once, before a match—he throws up right in my fuckin' face.

JS: [*laughs*]

GL: And, God, purple stuff came out.

JS: Ugh.

GL: And I said, "Bullshit," and then I jumped out of the ring, and I'm wiping this shit off me, and I'm really pissed, and I said, "Well, if the referee gives me a quick count, I'd start to get sick to my stomach, too."

JS: [*laughs*]

GL: And they counted me out, and he got a win. And he put it in his book, and I don't know, I might have put it in my book. I always tease him. "You crossed me. I hate it." But it's true, goddamn it. Roddy's a love. I really like him.

JS: Because I don't think a lot of people know that he's actually a legit guy.

GL: Yeah, and he's kind of from the old school. I saw him on a show. They were talking about putting down pro wrestling. He showed his wrist, where it was busted and it didn't heal right. He pulled down his pants and everything, and he said, "You think wrestling's easy? Get your ass in here. I'll wrestle you." He would, too.

JS: Yeah, I've met him once. He's a really sincere guy.

GL: Very, very nice guy. A class act. In my book that'll be out, he wrote a nice foreword.

JS: Oh, great.

GL: And so did Chuck. They don't get any better than Chuck. And of course, Bob Calhoun wrote a letter, and his letter is funny. He's got a great sense of humor.

JS: Oh, he was great. He was actually the backbone of the ISW [Incredibly Strange Wrestling] promotion I wrestled for. The promotion was only me and one other guy that had any kind of legit wrestling background. Everybody else were just comedians that knew how to take a bump, really. It was all funny gimmicks, and he would get on the mic, and he could get the crowd laughing so well.

GL: Yeah, he did my roast. He was one of the guys that roasted me. And it was funny, but it's an in-joke because I try not to put down people. In this book that was stolen from me [published without his full consent], they put down a couple of people. I was just talking to him, as I'm talking to you, and I don't put down people. I try not to.

JS: Yeah.

GL: I might say this guy's an asshole but you know he's a good guy. And even in my book I don't put down my brother, who's the biggest thief in the world. I just put a paragraph from Freddie's book saying that Gene was a great wrestler and his brother, maybe, had different parents because he'd steal for this and steal for that. And so it wasn't me that said my brother's an asshole thief, and Freddie didn't give a damn.

JS: Yeah, I think that's a great policy. No sense in hurting anybody.

GL: Well, being in show business stunts for 49 years ...

JS: Yeah.

GL: How's that for a quick calculation.

JS: Wow.

GL: You learn a lot of things. I've been with a lot of stars. I've seen a lot of things that I shouldn't have seen, and why bury them? My mother used to say this, and it's probably why I say it, "If you have to build yourself up by knocking somebody else, you're a loser yourself."

JS: Yeah, no sense in name calling anyone. Now, you were pretty close with Vic Christy, too.

GL: Very, very close.

JS: He was a tough guy.

GL: He was a very good wrestler, very underestimated wrestler. He hooked a lot of guys. I remember years ago, in the early '50s, Lou and Baron Leone were going to have a match at Gilmore Stadium, or whatever it was. A big match. So Lou had to work with five or six guys and beat them really quick, and Vic got behind him and hooked him and rode him, and this is like a five-minute workout. So he got him, hooked him, and Lou wants to, at the end of the match, be winning—like he could win—make it look like everybody was easy. So he got behind him for the last two minutes and held him. Well, if somebody is not as good as you—and Vic was very good—gets you in a hold and you can't get out of it, it's tough. So the bell rang, and Vic got up and ran out of the arena . . .

JS: [*laughs*]

GL: . . . Which is kind of interesting. And, of course, Lou wanted to kill him. Vic used to do all these things. He got my ass thrown in jail. I'm in Texas and this son of a bitch—well, it's a long story.

We're in this town. You go from one town to another. The guys are in their own cars. To make a long story short, they all stayed at this fleabag hotel, and you stayed for a dollar a day or something. You go down the hall to the bathroom. Doc Sarpolis was a hooker then, and he was a promoter. In this small town, I start to go. I have my two suitcases, my clothes. We're on the road. We live in Amarillo, but we stay overnight for three days in San Angelo, Abilene, and Lubbock. So I go down, and there's a couple of guys in brown cop uniform, and Vic's there on his knees.

"I can't help it. He's a kleptomaniac." And I said, "What the fuck is he talking about, a kleptomaniac? And I'm not even thinking of a practical joke but that's all he did, play jokes on me.

JS: [*laughs*]

GL: And the cop comes up to me and gives me a shove, and he said, "What have you got in your bags?" And I said, "This is my clothes and my wrestling gear. I'm a professional wrestler, and I'm leaving to go to Amarillo" or some other town along the way. "Why, what's the problem, officer?" And he said, "Well, we've had trouble here. Open up the suitcase." And I said, "You open it up." He opens it up, and there's sheets and towels and a bible.

JS: [*laughs*]

GL: I said, "I don't know. That's my clothes." He said, "What's in the other suitcase?" I said, "My wrestling gear." And about this time, I was wondering if Vic did something. Vic crawls over to the guy, grabs him on the leg, and he's crying, hysterically. "He's a kleptomaniac. He doesn't know what he's doing." And I said, "Hey, Vic. I'm the main event, here, on the next town. Don't screw me up." The cop opens up this bag. I don't know where the wrestling gear was. There was a [roll of] toilet paper, the Gideon Bible . . .

JS: [*laughs*]

GL: . . . And some feathers from somewhere, probably a pillow or something. And Vic said, "You're going to jail." I said, "I'm not going to jail. I'm going to wrestle. Where's my gear?" And there's Christy crying on the ground. "Don't take him away. His mother loves him. We love him," and all this shit.

JS: [*laughs*]

GL: And off I go. My wallet *was* in the suitcase, and I said to the cop, "Look, my wallet's in the suitcase. I don't know how much gas I have in the car. Can you give me $10?" He said, "Get the fuck out of here. If I see you in this town again, you're going to jail forever." So I went to my car, and I said, "If I run out of gas, I'm dead."

I go into the next town, and I see on the little marquee there, "Judo Gene Wrestling the Baron." Well, that's the name he worked under at that time, the Baron. And I said, "This son of a bitch. I'm going to fuck him up really good." I walk in the dressing room, and there are my clothes, my wallet, and some wrestling things (a couple of my clothes were gone, a T-shirt, which about a month later I see Vic wearing, and he went, "No, this was given to me by one of the wrestlers"). I said, "I'm going to fuck this son of a bitch. I'm going to kill his ass." And [Vic] gets in the ring, and this is the main event. There's maybe 300 people in the arena, if there was that many. He goes for a headlock. I go behind him, I pick his ass up as high as I could, backwards, and drop him on the back of his head.

JS: [*laughs*]

GL: I figure, "Well, we're going to have fun for a while," but it knocked him out. And I did a nelson and cranked him up pretty good. His eyes were rolled back. Then I got up, went to the dressing room, and I took off. Halfway back we stopped at this eating place. I think I put this in the book, but it's a funny story anyway. It was really great. They used to make home cooking, mom's home cooking, and they had big, fluffy biscuits. They used to make hamburger steaks, big, round hamburger steaks with baked potatoes and garden fresh vegetables. I mean, after wrestling you stop in this town. It was not expensive, and they had the best soups that you've ever tasted. Hunks of meat in them. So I go in, and I'm sitting on a stool, and two of the guys that were in the preliminaries are there, and they nod. But it's on television, the heels and the baby faces don't talk to each other.

JS: Right.

GL: And so they're looking, and it's raining hard, and the door swings open, and here comes a guy, all full of mud, in a suit. And it's Vic. He comes and sits at a stool, right next to me, mud all over his body. I'm thinking, "Oh, God. I screwed him up because I couldn't take a swerve. I'm a prick. I'm an asshole. I'll never do it again. What can I do to do the right thing?"

JS: [laughs]

GL: And so I'm looking at him. He takes his time. The gal comes up and says, "What do you want to eat?" Now you've got to see, all around the top are these different signs, "Jesus Loves You," and all those very religious things.

JS: Okay, okay.

GL: He's there, and he said, "Waaa" [makes whining noise]. I'm trying to help him out. He wants some soup, and he finally said, "Soup."

JS: [laughs]

GL: I'm there, and I'm thinking, "Oh my goodness. I don't know what to do." And these other two guys, who are wrestlers, are looking at me. Art Nelson was one of them. I forget who the other guy was. They think it's a shoot. I do too. Of course, it was. So he tries to pick up this big spoon and to eat the soup. He can't pick it up, and he's trying, and he starts to have hysterics. He can't pick up the spoon. He begins to try to pick up the bowl, and he's still part of it, and she said, "Wait a minute." I think he's working, [but] I didn't want to take a chance. I said, "Excuse me, lady. I'll feed him," and she pinched me on the forearm, and it hurt! And she said, "There but for the grace of God go you!"

JS: [laughs]

GL: So she feeds him the bowl, and it's going down his face. I mean, it's all over the place. I really felt like I did something, and, God forgive me, you've got to see it in person. And then he said, "Ah, ah, ah. Hahhh! How much? How much? Howww muchhh?" So she said, "25 cents." It's a big bowl of soup. I mean, it's a dinner in itself. So he's reaching in his pocket. I'm reaching in my pocket because I'm going to pay for it. I start to get close, and she doesn't look at me. She looks at him in the eye and shoves my arm away. "Get out of here." And he finally goes into this thing where you keep your watches in a double-breasted suit, and he pulls out a quarter, a muddy, dirty, old, wet quarter. He's looking at it really close to make sure it's a quarter, not a nickel. Then she's reaching her hand out, shaking, to grab it. He flips it in the air, grabs it, and slams it on the counter there and says, "That's the best damn service I've ever had."

JS: [*laughs*]

GL: And I fell over, off the chair because it had no back on it. I hit my head and hurt myself, and the wrestlers thought I was just working. I said, "Oh, my God. He's alive." He fucked me, and I just fell off. I can't explain it. I'm in my 20s. What did I know? Early 20s. Off he goes, out the door.

JS: Oh, that's funny.

GL: Yeah, it's funny. It ain't funny when you're there. So that went on all my life. When Vic was retired I moved to the condo where I'm at now. And he's out in the park, across the street—this is before they built the small fence—and he's in a jockstrap, sunbathing. He did that lots of times.

JS: Oh my God!

GL: And I look out, and I thought, "That's Vic," and I said to my wife, "Look at that degenerate freak there in a bikini bathing suit. He's a pervert, right in the middle of the parking lot." It's right across the street. You could see it. I said, "I'm going over there and talk to him." And she said, "Don't you dare."

So I drive over there in my car because I have to take off. She wasn't going to come with me, but she wanted to make sure I didn't say anything. So I get out of the car, and I said, "Get the hell out of this park, you sick degenerate." And the jockstrap is like a bathing suit that you wear underneath your wrestling gear sometimes. I said, "Get out of here." And he said, "Well, I'm getting rays. I'm getting rays." And she said, "Gene, get back in the car," and we get out of there.

JS: [laughs]

GL: So she screamed at me for a couple of days. Opened the door and there was Vic, sitting in a chair. Right at the door. He rang the doorbell and sat there, and he said, "You got a nickel for dinner or a quarter for dinner?"

JS: [laughs]

GL: And I said, "It's that same fuckin' degenerate. Don't talk like that." Things went like that. He always did things like that. When we'd go out to eat, he'd say, "Well, I'm going to buy," and of course I'd end up with the check some fucking way.

Before he got sick he did extra work. He wanted to go to the actors' home because they take real good care of you and they weren't charging at that time. He tried for six months. He knew a lot of big movie stars, but they couldn't get him into the Screen Actors Guild home.

I used to hire him because I was running stunts. I hired him on *California Split*. He was an extra and I was a stunt guy, and they wanted somebody to throw a punch at an actor, which was me. I thought, "Oh, he'll throw a nice, working punch," and he did it, and I thought, "Well, everything's okay. He didn't try to cause trouble." He's over with the director, telling him I'm a screaming fag, that I shouldn't be on the set, and he's going to run the stunts from now on in all his movies.

JS: [laughs]

GL: Then the first assistant comes up to me, and he said, "Well, the director doesn't like fags," and I said, "So? What's that have to do with me?" So that went on.

JS: Oh my gosh.

GL: I mean, that went on for years, but when he got sick—he lived only a mile from here. A couple of times he fell out of bed. He called me up, and I had to go over and pick him up, to put him back in bed. Undress him. I called a doctor friend of mine who worked at the actors' home. I said, "Do you know anybody that has enough clout to get a guy in?" And he said, "Geez, it's impossible. But I've got a guy there that will probably die within a day or two, and I'll see what I can do." The guy died the next day, and he shoved Vic in there.

JS: Wow.

GL: So he was there for a few months. I used to visit him every other day. The day before he died, I went there. He was in a depression. His legs had turned purple because of lack of circulation. He had cancer and every other damn thing, and he said, "I'm going to die." And I said, "No, you're not going to die because I just talked to a doctor and he's moving you to one of these outside bungalows in a couple of days, and, boy, it'll be really nice there." And he was really happy, and he said, "I want you to get a picture of you and your wife, and we're going to pin it on the wall." I'm trying to make him happy . . .

JS: Yeah.

GL: . . . And everything like that because he was a big part of my life. I went back the next day, and they said he'd just passed away.

JS: Oh.

GL: And that was a tearjerker.

JS: Yeah. So you guys were really close.

GL: Oh, yeah. He wanted to be next to Ted. He had a plot of ground. His nephews got the money and had him cremated and sold the plot. I don't know. They might be really good guys. I never talked to them about it, but a couple of the wrestlers were teed off. I mean, the guy changed my life. Everybody you meet changes your life.

JS: Yeah.

GL: Some of these stories I put in the book. I mean, he did more things to me. He got me into wrestling. I used to work out. My name was LeBell, and my mother married my stepdad, named Eaton. Everybody knew Cal Eaton. They didn't know Aileen Eaton was my mother. I was just a wrestler. I used to work out a couple of days a week at the Legion, where they'd try to teach guys how to work. They did a little bit of shooting and a little bit of working, so I was having fun. I said I wanted to be a wrestler, but my stepdad doesn't want me to be. [Vic] didn't know who my stepdad was. So the long and short of it, Jules Strong-bow comes in. I'm wrestling some guys that are pretty good wrestlers, good amateur wrestlers, and I'm playing with them, and he said, "Great, this guy, Jules and Cal Eaton, they're the promoters. They're coming down to the ring right now. If you want to be a pro wrestler, that's the guy." I went through the rope. My stepdad said he'd kill me if I was ever training with the pro wrestlers at Main Street Gym. And, of course, I lived at Main Street Gym with the pro wrestlers, so I got out.

My dad and I, before, had a bet. He said, "If you want to be a pro wrestler, I've got a guy—he's named Louie Miller—that's not as big as you, and he'll stretch you five times in five minutes." And I said, "Well, bet me." He was really a frustrated bully. So we bet $100. And he said, "I'm going to take it from you, too," and he always treated me like garbage.

So a week later I said, "Did you call this Louie Miller up to set up our wrestling match?" And he said, "Don't bother me." I knew what happened. He went to talk to Louie—because Louie was a good wrestler—but I'd been working out with Louie for three or four years.

So Cal said, "Okay. You want to be a wrestler. We're going to start you." And I said, "That's great, but I can't wrestle right now because I'm training for the '55 nationals." And he said, "That's two months."

I was in the top shape of my life. A lot of people said I had won the last one on luck, and I was going to prove that it wasn't luck. So a week before, I come down with the worst tonsillitis in the world. He said, "I told you. You don't enter this tournament." I said, "I'm going to enter it no matter what."

Well, the long and the short of it is, where was the tournament? Held in Los Angeles. What did the Amateur Athletic Union rent? The Olympic Auditorium, from my mother, and Cal didn't know anything about it.

JS: Oh my gosh.

GL: So I'm there. I come in with a 104° [40°C] temperature.

JS: Oh my God.

GL: It's a two-day tournament, and he's really given me a vote of confidence: "You dumb son of a bitch." I made it to the second day. I was pretty lucky, you know, but I was running out of gas. I couldn't eat. One of the guys from the United States Air Force, one of the training guys, gave me an orange, a big orange, and it gave me such a lift, a sugar rush, that the next few matches ... I had 18 matches in two days.

JS: Ugh.

GL: And that's a lot. Now, the way the rules are, you get four or five matches in amateur judo and you've won the nationals. So a one-day tournament. They had a point system that you really had to be good or damn lucky, as I was. So it goes on and on, then he wanted me to turn pro. I said, "I can't," because if you win you go for the internationals in Japan. Of course, I had this tonsil trouble, and I couldn't eat. I get down to 163 pounds [74 kg]. I look like a polio victim with a six-pack. It went on and on. I never did get along with Cal.

JS: But so, then, how did Vic play into that, in terms of you getting started?

GL: Oh, well, Vic told him, "Hey, we've got all these good shooters in there, and Gene hooks them all. And easy." He said, "You've got to get this guy," and Vic didn't know that I was related to Cal. In fact, Vic was showing him a body slam. I used to take good bumps, and he showed him how he could body slam me. I used to do a gimmick where they'd slam me and my feet would hit the ropes and I'd do a flip, completely over, and land on my back and the guy would top me. It's just a comedy thing. I guess they saw that earlier. Then we went into some shooting. So, Cal always said if I wrestled every other pro would beat me up. He never saw me wrestle, so he didn't know how good I was. I used to work out with Joe Pazandak, who was a good shooter.

Gene LeBell is a legend, and I thank goodness that he did what he did for grappling here in the United States. Visit his website, www.GeneLe Bell.com, to learn more about him.

★★★ JOSH BARNETT (1977–) ★★★

JOSH HAS LONG BEEN a huge advocate of my research and work with catch-as-catch-can. Before anyone had heard the term "catch-as-catch-can," Josh was championing it in the competitive arena—and winning! What follows is an interview with the former UFC heavyweight champion, a much-feared competitor.

JAKE SHANNON: How did you meet Billy Robinson?

JOSH BARNETT: I met Billy through the UWF Snake Pit. I was told about the gym through some friends (Gryphon, I think) and really wanted to check it out. At the time, Oe-san and Miyato-san were the only ones there, but Miyato-san told me all about Billy and that I should be sure to come when Billy is in. While I lived in Japan, every time I was in Tokyo I would go to the UWF Snake Pit to train, and Billy worked with me a lot. I trained there for many of my fights, with

Oe-san training my striking and Billy with Miyato-san improving my wrestling skills.

JS: What was the first meeting like? What did you do and talk about?

JB: I didn't know what to expect, but he had a very high reputation, so I felt very strongly about wanting to learn from him. First things first, besides an introduction, I got to know Billy by getting on the mat and wrestling! He taught many finer points to the double and top wrist-lock that night, showed me what I call the "Billy Neck Crank," and coached me and Miyato-san as we wrestled.

JS: Please explain your passion for catch wrestling.

JB: It's a root on the tree of MMA. Catch went to Brazil with Mitsuyo Maeda, formed the basis of New Japan Pro Wrestling and later Japanese shooting through Gotch and Billy, and was an art based on battle testing. It's aggressive and explosive and has a deep history throughout the world and was my first major exposure to submission.

One of the reasons I got into MMA was because of pro wrestling. I always knew that pro wrestling was a sport of real tough men and that most people only knew the surface of pro wrestling. I get upset to see that something like catch, that used to be known and popular all throughout the world, is being ignored. Catch was here before BJJ, and BJJ is not the end-all, be-all of submissions. I will bring catch wrestling back to the forefront and in the limelight again, and I'll do it by beating my opponents.

JS: Who are your top three favorite catch-as-catch-can wrestlers of all time?

JB: Billy Robinson and Karl Gotch for bringing catch to Japan and creating the people that would revolutionize pro wrestling/MMA. Ad Santel for declaring war against the best judokas and showing catch wrestlers were among the strongest wrestlers in the world.

JS: What do you think of the current state of catch, and what can be done to improve it?

JB: Some people say catch is a dying or esoteric art. While I don't think it's coming to the forefront, it is on, making its presence felt again. There are some folks like myself and Megumi Fujyii, to name a few, that are actively competing, but, unfortunately, there are not enough of us out there. Competition is the only way to truly promote the art and increase its awareness.

I think catch would be much better suited to bringing amateur wrestlers to MMA, as well. I see many top amateur wrestlers go to BJJ gyms because that's what they think you have to train to learn submission. Most of the time though, those BJJ trainers train the wrestlers in ways that are counterproductive to a wrestler's skills and strengths. Everyone needs a game off their back, but not everyone has to use a guard game like a BJJ player.

With active competitors out there in MMA and submission wrestling representing catch, it is the only way we can spread the art. Seeing winners out there using catch will make that person who might not have known about catch make the decision to go to a gym and learn to wrestle and not sit on their butts.

JS: What is your opinion on the demise of the Pride Fighting Championships?

JB: The loss of Pride's rules, judging, and our ability to wear shoes or *dogis* are a tragic loss to MMA. I am very upset about this and wish people did not try to marginalize our ability to fight and perform in the ring/cage. It is really disturbing that, 90 percent of the time, these rules and regulations come from people who've never fought.

JS: What are your plans in the short term for your mixed martial arts career?

JB: Become number one. If you aren't trying to be the best than why do it? We may never become the best, but without trying you will never know.

JS: What do you see yourself doing 20 years from now?

JB: Running my own successful dojo and promotion and enjoying my cars, I hope!

JS: When will you do pro wrestling again? Would you ever consider working for the WWE?

JB: Perhaps. It is a big stage, and it would be great to use it to show what I believe is pro wrestling, but it is really hard to say at this point. I loved working in New Japan, and one of my real passions is to make a new type of UWF. I am not forever removed from pro wrestling and will be in the ring again, I promise.

JS: What do you think of the influential shoot-style professional wrestling matches featuring Antonio Inoki versus Muhammad Ali and Inoki versus Acram Peru I (Great Gama Family)?

JB: I think Inoki versus Ali was a historical match-up that helped pro wrestling's popularity a lot, but it was not much of a match because the wrestler really couldn't wrestle. The rules were much too restrictive for Inoki, and he was, in my opinion, handicapped by them. If the match was Pride rules, Inoki would have beaten Ali easily and quickly.

Inoki versus Acram showed that just because you have famous family name it doesn't mean you are as great as they were. Acram asked for the match to be a shoot, insisted to do it his way, and Inoki said, "Okay, we can fight any way you want." Inoki had someone backstage hit him in the face a few times, and then Inoki went out to the ring and put a real hurt on Acram. In the end, Acram got more than he asked for when Inoki broke his arm with a double wristlock.

JS: Have you been able to train with Antonio Inoki while you were wrestling for New Japan Pro Wrestling?

JB: I have not been able to work out much with Inoki-sama, but he has shown me a few techniques and spent a lot of time talking with me. I have been very lucky to have received much advice from Inoki-sama. Much of what I do in pro wrestling is what Inoki-sama has tried to teach me along with people like Miyato-san and Liger, to name a few that have taught me.

JS: What is the most impressive match in Inoki's repertoire?

JB: Inoki versus Billy Robinson is the template for a pro wrestling match, and I think all aspiring wrestlers should watch it to learn from it.

JS: Do you have any particularly interesting memories with Inoki that stand out in your mind?

JB: Speaking one-on-one with Inoki-sama before my match against Scott Norton at the Green Dome in Sapporo. His support of me and talking about our beliefs in pro wrestling was a strong moment for me.

JS: What do you think Mr. Inoki's legacy will be?

JB: Inoki-sama is an icon to professional wrestling and spokesperson for the truth of real, strong pro wrestling. I will always be grateful to Inoki-sama for his building up of pro wrestling and contributions to MMA.

JS: What is your impression of the present ADCC [Abu-Dhabi Combat Club] fighters?

JB: Too much holding and point playing and not enough submission and takedown game. Most of the time, when you watch two good grapplers at ADCC it is boring, with lots of stalling. A match between top guys should be the most exciting!

JS: In Pride, you could wear wrestling shoes or a judo *gi*. What do you think of the UFC's elimination of this optional gear?

JB: Not being able to wear a *dogi* or wrestling shoes is nonsense!

JS: How about the first round at ten minutes and following rounds at five minutes structure?

JB: I like the ten-minute round, but the most important thing was the Pride judging system. I believe it covers the bout as a whole better than the current U.S. systems do.

JS: What do you think would be the best "dream matches" for your fans?

JB: A rematch with Randy Couture, even though I've already beat him. It wouldn't have to be for the belt either. I think a dream match-up for me is Volk Han or maybe Alexander Karelin. Of course, those are truly "what if" matches, but I think the fans would love them. If U-style were still around, I would want a rematch with Tamura-san and to get TK out of retirement for just one match. It would be amazing!

★ ★ ★ ERIK PAULSON (1966–) ★ ★ ★

MORE PEOPLE SHOULD KNOW ABOUT Erik Paulson. He has done much for catch-as-catch-can. He's not as a purist, but he has taken Bruce Lee's concept of taking what works in martial arts and discarding the rest and created his own hybrid style that features Brazilian jujitsu, Muay Thai kickboxing, and other styles in equal measure with catch-as-catch-can. As such, Erik has been an ambassador who has opened people's minds to the effective and tough style of catch-as-catch-can submission grappling.

JAKE SHANNON: Maybe we should start by talking about your introduction to catch-as-catch-can. What were you doing before you did it? And then when were you first introduced and how did it change your thoughts about grappling and wrestling?

ERIK PAULSON: I was a gymnast in high school. I started judo in

1974. My brother was a wrestler, and I started karate in 1976 in Minnesota. I dealt with a bunch of wrestlers all the time because they always wanted to fight or, at least, come into our karate school and train or workout or sometimes watch.

I really got my first taste of catch wrestling, I think, probably, with Larry Hartsell. When I first met Larry in 1982, he was doing a Smoky Mountain camp. He was in Minnesota, originally, with Rick Faye. And then I did a camp in 1985. We did a camp called the martial arts camp. I got trained with him, and he was showing a lot of the cool takedowns and neck cranks that he got from Gene LeBell and from Bruce Lee and Dan Inosanto.

JS: For those who don't know who Larry Hartsell is, he was kind of a big name in the Jeet Kune Do movement, right? And then he learned a lot of the catch from Gene, and he was based out in Los Angeles. He recently passed away, isn't that correct?

EP: Yes, he just died, just died two years ago. But he was the one that actually turned me on to the grappling. He said, "You know, when all technique is equal, your strength will prevail, so start lifting weights and start grappling all the time," he goes, "because your option and ability to get into grappling is going to happen every single real fight you're going to get into."

JS: And this was back in, you said, like, the late '80s, early '90s?

EP: I'm sorry, say that again?

JS: When you were first having Hartsell tell you some of this stuff and first getting turned on to the catch-as-catch-can, this was, like, the late '80s, early '90s. Is that fair?

EP: Yes. Yeah, it was '82 through until the time he died, and I met and trained with him for a while, and then . . . I know what happened. I ended up hooking up with Yori Nakamura, training with Yori and Gene LeBell, also.

JS: And Yori came from the Shooto organization, isn't that correct?

EP: He came from Shooto. He learned from Sayama, and Sayama was trained by Karl Gotch.

JS: And then, for those who don't know about Shooto, what are the rules and the time period when that was going on, because it's a Japanese fight promotion?

EP: First amateur was 1984 until present. They've actually had the most MMA fights in history, as far as all the organizations. It was actually one of the first sanctioned MMA events. The fights were in '84 all the way up until now, and they still have a new organization called Vale Tudo Japan.

JS: What's the name of the new promotion again?

EP: Vale Tudo Japan. In Vale Tudo Japan, they allow soccer kicks on the ground and stomps. I don't think they allow elbows. I don't think they allow head butts because Japan doesn't really like the blood, but they still allow the soccer kick and the punt, and the rounds are a lot longer. Well, before the rounds were eight-minute rounds. Three eight-minute rounds. I'm not quite sure what their rounds are today.

JS: Interesting.

EP: Yeah, they're just trying to make it a little more real.

JS: And then you went on to actually win the championship. Was it middleweight or light heavyweight?

EP: I was light heavyweight.

JS: So you were the light heavyweight champion for shooto. How long was that? Tell me a little bit about it.

EP: I got it in '96, '95. I kept it until 2000. Actually, in 2001 I got rid of it. I retired, and I had two other belts. I had two of the belts from Japan, and I retired as the champion, the reigning two-time champ.

JS: Wonderful, very cool.

EP: And I never lost to a Japanese guy. Maybe that's why I have a Japanese haters club there.

JS: So you had done some grappling before you had done the catch-as-catch-can, or not at all?

EP: Well, just wrestling with my brother and judo.

JS: Oh, okay. So you were already doing catch-as-catch-can before kind of the whole Brazilian jujitsu craze caught on here in the United States.

EP: Yeah, with Larry . . . But it wasn't quite as established as it is right now. It's established now, but it was just bits and pieces back then, and the thing that really helped was the explosion of the UFC and the Gracies coming in and actually teaching people all about positioning.

JS: I think that's one of the great things that I've really appreciated about the role that you've played. You've been able to kind of bridge both gaps because you still kind of keep to that Jeet Kune Do philosophy of just taking whatever works and throwing away what doesn't. And as such, you do both Brazilian jujitsu and the catch-as-catch-can. You kind of blend it into your own unique style, and that's the combat submission wrestling, right?

EP: One helps the other. When I first learned all the combinations, all the catch combos from shooto, it's combos one through ten. There's 150 locks. But the thing with the jujitsu is it teaches you how to transition and actually put them together, how to flow and blend a little more, I think, because of their transitions. They're really big, obviously, into the guard, into the sweeps, into the development of guard passing. And for a catch wrestler to say, "Oh, you know, the guard, it's just a completely invaluable position, very invaluable and it's just not. . . ." Most of the guys that you're going to fight, that have jujitsu, are going to submit you from the guard.

JS: And I agree with that 100 percent. I think there's a lot of, kind of, silly nonsense between people who like catch-as-catch-can and people who like Brazilian jujitsu. And like I said, what I like about you is you do them both, and you take what you like from each particular . . .

EP: Right. I add the submissions. I add the cranks. I add the little tweaks from catch wrestling to the jujitsu, and it develops [into] a different animal. You know, you're like, "Wow. That's weird," but you move differently. You move more like a wrestler, and then if I go with a wrestler, then I go straight to jujitsu. Like when I went to the Snake Pit and I wrestled with Billy's little guy there. What's his name? Miyato?

JS: Oh, Miyato. The Japanese wrestler, right.

EP: Yeah, Miyato. I wrestled with him, and we started on our knees, and I couldn't take him down. We were going for 15 minutes on our knees. And, finally, I'm like, heck with that, so I pulled guard, and then I swept him. And that's the strategy I had to use because I couldn't beat him in the wrestling aspect because his wrestling, his hand fighting, was so good.

JS: Yeah, so you take the strengths of one, kind of based upon who your opponent is and what their strengths are.

EP: Yeah. Your gain has to change depending on every guy you're going with. But one thing I like is that all the catch locks are so aggressive. They're very deliberate, and it's all basically based on ripping something out, cranking it, and tearing it. It's very aggressive and their style is very ballistic.

JS: Which maybe lends itself better to competition, where if you're going to get it, you've got to take it when you can get it.

EP: And it's also a little more turbo. Someone said, "What's jujitsu ground fighting compared to shooto ground fighting?" I go, "Well, obviously the positions are a lot more acknowledged in jujitsu, but the attacking mentality of shooto, which is like catch, is all jujitsu on steroids."

JS: Now, let me ask you this, because of, like you said, the UFC and the Gracies' involvement with UFC early on, it seems like you see a Brazilian jujitsu school in every strip mall these days. What do you think is required for catch-as-catch-can to get that same sort of following? Is it mostly just education or . . .

EP: What's going to happen is there's going to be such an oversaturation of jujitsu that people are all going to say, "Well, everyone's a black belt jujitsu." When I went in, a blue belt was like a black belt. Now there's so many guys getting their black belts that they've oversaturated the market. Now catch wrestling is going to be the newest go-to grappling system that a lot of guys are going to want to start learning. That's like Eddie Bravo's system. Because it's different than most jujitsu styles, a lot of guys are turning and trying to learn his system of the half rubber guard, you know, that style of jujitsu with the half guard and rubber guard.

JS: Which almost speaks to exactly what you're talking about. Like if you fight a jujitsu guy, you want to do something different than jujitsu. You want to do a catch wrestling or maybe an Eddie Bravo style or something unorthodox.

EP: Or you want to have scrambles and be aggressive and really be able to try to use your wrestling and stuff.

JS: Yeah, that makes sense. And for the people who may not know, you're a fight trainer. You've really built quite a reputation and a career around training high-level fighters, like Josh Barnett. Who are some of the other guys that you've trained?

EP: I've helped Ken Shamrock, Guy Mezger, Vernon White. I helped Sean Sherk. I helped Dave Monet. I helped Brock Lesner. I've helped Babilu, Harvey Vasquez, James Wilks, Ben Jones, Jim Martinez, Craig Wilkerson, Cub Swanson. I've worked and helped a lot of these different fighters with their game development and also to have more of a well-rounded system when they're fighting. When they're good at grappling, they're good at attacking, good at striking, and good at takedowns.

JS: You also credit working a little bit with Gene LeBell in learning a few things.

EP: I turn to Gene as much as I can, whenever I get a chance. Gene's got a ton of information. He's a catch wrestler that a lot of guys . . . there should be a movie or something. Gene doesn't get the notoriety that he should, as far as catch wrestling goes because he's, you know, judo . . .

JS: Yeah, his whole marketing has been around Judo Gene LeBell, but I've gone and trained with him a little bit, too, and he's really amazing. He's got so many different finishing holds, it's crazy.

EP: Yeah, as far as, like, submission, he's got tons of great steps.

JS: And now he's got one of his guys, Neil Melanson—who's also seen the benefits that working in some catch-as-catch-can can give—training Randy Couture and some of these other guys to give them an edge, as well. So it seems like people are kind of following your footsteps in terms of being more open-minded and incorporating some of the moves of catch-as-catch-can, which is great. In that way, you're kind of like a godfather of that cross-training style that's now bringing out the real, authentic catch-as-catch-can, the stuff that actually plays out well in competition.

EP: I think that's the next step. I think it's very applicable for the UFC and for all these MMA events. And you're finding a lot of the guys that are crossing over now are a lot of the pro wrestlers from Japan because Pride fell through, and a lot of the guys, like Minowa and some of these other Japanese fighters, they've all got a background in pro wrestling and catch wrestling.

JS: Let me ask you something, if there was anything that you wanted to communicate about catch-as-catch-can to a broader audience, what is it that you would say? What would you like to get across?

EP: Well, it's not anything new. It's just new to people who are finding it now. It's ancient, you know? A lot of the old American submission wrestlers were using a lot of these holds from the early 1900s. They learned from some of these guys, and it's been passed down for countless decades to many different pro wrestlers, real fighters, MMA fighters, carnival wrestling, and now submission wrestling events. Earlier leg locks were looked down upon, wristlocks were looked down upon, neck cranks weren't even allowed. Now, they're starting to allow some of these locks that are very predominant from catch wrestling.

JS: Thank you for not only taking the time, but for everything that you've done and that you continue to do to keep catch-as-catch-can having a good reputation and being a positive thing for people to explore and practice and have fun with. I just wanted to thank you for that.

EP: My pleasure. Thank you.

★ ★ ★ MARK FLEMING (1962–) ★ ★ ★

MARK FLEMING BEGAN WRESTLING at the age of 13. He eventually won a high school championship in wrestling, and then he immediately began working as a pro wrestler. As a wrestler, Mark has participated in 19 tours of Japan (including a match against Antonio Inoki in the New Japan Pro Wrestling promotion). At one point Mark was ranked number two in the famous UWFi promotion. The real, true living protégé of Lou Thesz, Mark Fleming was managed by Thesz for seven years and was also the head coach at Thesz's wrestling gym for three years. Mark currently runs Fleming's Gym in downtown Portsmouth, Virginia. The following interview with Mark took place when he first opened his gym.

JAKE SHANNON: Well, I'm going to send as many people as I possibly can out there. Are you going to put any of the wrestling memorabilia stuff up?

MARK FLEMING: Oh, yeah. I've got a lot of it up already—a lot of pictures of the old guys, some of me wrestling in Japan, some of the other guys that I knew, that have autographed pictures for me. I've got those hanging up. A lot of people like all that stuff. People ask a lot of questions about it and all that. I always wanted to be a professional wrestler. It was a childhood dream. And, of course, everybody, all your friends and all, say you'll never make it.

Well, I went out for the wrestling team when I was 13 years old. I went and talked to my wrestling coach at the high school. Of course, I was too young as I wasn't in high school yet, but he liked my size. I was big for my age at 13, and he invited me to come out there and work out with the high school boys because I was only in seventh grade. I went out there and started working out with the high school kids. Finally, ninth grade came around. I earned my position on varsity.

JAKE: Wow.

MF: I did pretty well. The first year I got third in what they called the eastern district around here and, eventually, became the champion in my senior year. Wrestling didn't come easy for me. It was something I had to work at. I don't think I was really what they call a "natural."

JS: Yeah.

MF: I just lifted weights and was always conscious of it, even on the off-season. I entered all the summer tournaments. My coach used to tell me that he knew he could rely on me because I was one of the guys that he knew was always working towards it. I wasn't goofing off and doing all the things other kids do, like smoking and drinking and all that. I just always strived to become a professional wrestler, that was always my dream, and I told myself, if I didn't win the championship my senior year that I wouldn't even try it.

JS: Wow.

MF: So anyway, I won. And then I wrote a letter to one of the wrestling promoters here in North Carolina, and I told him I wanted to be a pro wrestler. I wrote a résumé of all the medals I'd won in Virginia. He wrote me back saying he knew the wrestling coach at UNC, the University of North Carolina, and that he'd drop my name to him, see if I can wrestle at the school there, at the college. Now, I didn't want that. I wanted to be a professional wrestler. I wasn't interested in going to college. So by going to the matches and watching these guys, I became pretty good friends with a guy named Ricky Steamboat.

JS: Yeah, of course.

MF: And by just talking to him on the sidelines, there, and just getting him to talk to me, or any of them to talk to me, I became pretty good friends with them. They knew who I was, and we'd talk about amateur wrestling. Finally Steamboat said, "Look. Give me your résumé of the tournaments and all you've won, and get some pictures taken of yourself, and I will submit them to the promoter. They have a tryout once a year, looking for new talent." He said, "I'll put it on his desk. I can't promise you anything, but you know how it goes. Just try it." So, gosh, about a year and a half went by. Finally they called me. They said, "Look, we've got a tryout, and we think you're good enough. Come on down to Charlotte, North Carolina, to the Coliseum and try out." When I get there—me and my dad went—there were like 24, 25 guys there. They were all college football players, college wrestlers. They had heard of me. I was like the third smallest guy there. I weighed 200 pounds [91 kg].

JS: [*laughs*]

MF: I was like, "Oh, gee, these guys are all big." We get in the ring with Ole Anderson, and he was rookie. We wrestle each other in a round-robin style. You know what that is?

JS: Sure.

MF: Eventually there was me and two other guys left. And I had pinned everybody that I wrestled. I don't know what in the world was wrong, but I just went crazy, and I just did an exceptionally good job. I was pinning everybody. Then he started paying attention to me. I and two other guys made the tryouts. They picked us. They sent us home, told us they'd give us a call back when they start training. It was almost about six months later when they called me back. I went down to Charlotte and trained. I had to catch a bus to keep going back down there because I didn't have a car that could make it. That went on for about a year, and I was trained by Ole and Gene Anderson. And, of course, they would bring in guys that would help us, other pros. We did this for about a year. It was some of the hardest workouts I'd ever seen in my life, I'd ever been through. Finally, the other two guys quit. One of them, they just told him he didn't have what it took. The other guy, that was a bodybuilder that could wrestle a little bit, he finally quit. I don't know what his deal was.

Anyway, they just kept up with me. Finally, one day, they told me that they were going to send me on the road with these guys. Of course, I got my ass kicked every night and all that, but I was riding with these guys and learning the ropes. That's when I was able to wrestle some of these older guys that were big names, years ago. Anyway, I worked for Crockett Promotions. I wrestled for them as a preliminary guy and wrestled these guys. I did it for, like, seven years. Finally they started giving me a little push, a little bit. They sent me to Kansas City, and I wrestled out in the Midwest.

JS: Now, while you were working for Crockett's, it was NWA, right?

MF: Yeah, that was the NWA.

JS: Is this when Lou Thesz took note of you?

MF: Believe it or not, he was living here in Norfolk. I knew this, but I was traveling so much, and I really hadn't had time to get up with him, and he didn't have anything to do with Crockett. He was out of wrestling completely then, but I had heard he lived here. One night, we were wrestling at the Scope Coliseum, which is here in Norfolk, and he came. Of course, I was in awe. He was sitting in the audience. He saw my match. After the matches were over, he came in the locker room and went around. Of course, all the big stars knew him. He was like a god.

JS: Yeah.

MF: And I went up and talked to him, and he said, "Yeah, kid, I saw your match. You can wrestle a little bit." I said, "Yeah," and I told him I wrestled amateur, and I said, "I try." He said, "Why don't you call me up some time? We'll get together, and I can show you some things."

So it just blossomed from there. He invited me to his house. We ate crabs. He lived right there on the Chesapeake Bay, right there on the beach. We sat down on the deck and ate crabs and talked about wrestling. He told me he thought he could help me, so we went to a gym here, locally, that had some wrestling mats. He showed me a couple of things.

JS: What kind of things did he show you?

MF: Oh, he showed me the double wristlock, stand and switch, reverse switch, just different things. He told me different ways I would look better doing stuff. He never really pushed it on me. He was just showing me, nonchalantly, and just saying, "You know, you can do this." He showed me the step-over toehold. And, just, repetitious. It wasn't a lot of holds, but he just kept showing me over and over and over. He just took a lot of time with me. And I'm thinking, "Why is this guy taking so much time with me? I'm just a preliminary guy. I'm not a big name." He said, "I've been thinking about starting up a wrestling school. I've got some interest in Japan sending some guys over here that I'll train." I said, "Well, that's cool. I'll be there."

So he brought some Japanese guys over. Of course, we went at it full speed and just wrestled. He would just teach us. None of the

Japanese guys could beat me. Finally, one day, he came up and said, "You know a lot about wrestling. You've really learned a lot of what I've showed you. I'd like for you to be my coach, here, at the wrestling school."

JS: Wow.

MF: I was still on the road wrestling, and he said, "I don't mean to tell you how to do your business or anything. This Crockett promotion thing, they're not treating you right. You're a better talent than how they're using you. But if you're happy in doing what you're doing, that's fine. But I'm just telling you that I think you've got more talent than what they're using you for." I took it as a compliment.

JS: Yeah, of course.

MF: So he started showing me the light, like how they're putting over these guys and building these guys up that have no wrestling ability whatsoever. He said, "Here you are. You're a good wrestler. You've got a good body. There's no reason why they won't build you up." Dusty Rhodes was in charge at the time. He was a booker, and [Lou] just told me the situation. He said, "Dusty Rhodes is not a wrestler. He's a fat showman," he said.

JS: [*laughs*]

MF: "He doesn't respect wrestlers." He said, "You're a different breed." In other words, he was trying to tell me that I'm not going to get anywhere with them because I wasn't doing the showmanship stuff, the steroids, the gimmicks, and all. You know what I'm saying?

JS: Yeah.

MF: He just told me, "I'll pay you," so he paid me. He hired me and paid me to teach at his school, which I did. And, also, he got me hooked up working at the gym where we lifted and all that. I eventually became manager of that gym.

JS: And you guys were close? He ended up being the best man at your wedding.

MF: Oh, we were together seven days a week. I would go to his house every day for lunch. He would feed me—not because I needed it. I had a great family and had plenty of money. It was just that he wanted me around, all the time. He would take me home. I would eat lunch with him every day in his house. He would invite me over on Sundays for Sunday dinner. Eventually, the girl that I was going to marry, my fiancée, he would invite us over. He would take us out. Oh yeah, we became real close. Anyway, he and I became real close, and, when I got married, Lou was my best man at my wedding. He was close to my family and all that. We were buddies. He was going to take me to Australia. He was working out a deal with a promoter for us to wrestle in, not a circus, but like a Busch Gardens.

JS: Like an amusement park?

MF: An amusement park. And we were going to put on two shows a day at this amusement park in Australia. It was going to be me, and Lou had a bunch of guys lined up. The promoter, at the last minute, cut our pay in half, and, Lou, he didn't take any funny business. He was like, "Screw you."

JS: I remember you telling me that Lou was a really amazing business-man. He really knew the money, right?

MF: Yup, he sure did. He didn't like anybody playing with him, as far as money or anything. If someone is trying to rip you off, he'll just tell you, he'll just blow you off. He won't give you a second chance. That's the way he was. He was hard-nosed when it came to business. But, you know, I was all pumped. I wanted to go, just because it was Australia, you know, and I was supposed to spend all summer there. We were going to spend all summer there. Lou wasn't even going, but he was handling all my affairs at the time, and he just told the guy, he said, "Cram it up your ass." He kind of messed it up for me. As a matter of fact, Lou had sent my wrestling tapes over there, and the guy never sent them back.

JS: Oh, that's so horrible, too.

MF: And I sent my masters.

JS: Oh, man.

MF: We had it all set. We were going, and I would get the tapes back, and the guy never sent them back.

JS: Oh, that sucks.

MF: I lost a lot of my tapes because of that, and it makes me sick, just thinking about it.

JS: And you didn't train under just Lou. I know you did a lot of stuff in Japan, too. Not only the worked matches, but like legit shoot stuff, too. I think it was when you were with UWFi, right? And you had, like, Danny Hodge and Billy Robinson out there.

MF: Yeah, well, when I was wrestling for Lou, there was a lot of Japanese guys coming to Virginia, here, to train under him. I don't know how it happened, but the UWF called for me to go over there and wrestle for them, about two years or three years, really, before I went with them. You ever heard of Maeda?

JS: Yeah.

MF: Maeda was in charge of it then. I guess he'd heard of me through these Japanese people . . . Oh, I know how it happened. It was an old wrestler by the name of Tokyo Joe. His name was Joe Daigo. You ever heard of him?

JS: No.

MF: He was an old Japanese wrestler, a wooden leg. He came over here to scout some of these Japanese guys that Lou and I were training. I caught his eye. He wanted me to go over there and wrestle on his shoot, like when it first started. It was Maeda that was in charge. Lou, of course, was getting a piece of my action because he was my man. I don't know what happened. I don't know if Lou didn't think I was ready or they weren't offering the right money. Anyway, it never happened.

So we were continuing to train Japanese guys. They even featured me in a shoot magazine over there. They gave me two pages in a shoot-like magazine in Japan, and I hadn't even gone over there yet. And, of course, something had happened because I walked into the middle of it at Lou's house. Him and Joe Daigo were arguing, and Lou took a wine glass and threw it in the sink. And he wouldn't ever tell me what it was about, and I don't know what it was about, but, anyhow, I didn't go over there.

So we continued training, and I was doing a little wrestling with independent groups around Virginia. It hadn't stopped at NWA. And, finally, Joe Daigo came back and offered me a contract with New Japan, Antonio Inoki's company, and that's more like a work.

JS: Yeah, right.

MF: It's more of a shoot than over here, but it's still a work.

JS: It's just a stiff work.

MF: Yeah, it's a very stiff work. So I went over there and stayed a month, wrestling for them, wrestling for Inoki. Came back and wrestled. Kept wrestling in independent groups around here in North Carolina. Still trained at Lou's place. Finally we had trouble with it. We had to move our school—the landlord or something like that—and Lou brought this guy over. He had another scout from a shoot-like company. What was this guy's name? Odjio? You ever hear of Odjio?

JS: No. I don't know. I haven't heard of him either.

MF: He was a student of Fujiwara. You know Fujiwara?

JS: Oh, yeah, I know Fujiwara. So he was one of Fujiwara's students?

MF: Well, he was wrestling for Fujiwara, and he came, and we were wrestling. We were practicing at a boxing gym by then. But he came out and watched me work out. He brought a wrestler named Cinji with him. He was supposed to be some bad-ass. Well, I tore his ass up. He was a smart-ass. He was real cocky, and he was a smart-ass. He was supposed to be some great wrestler and all this shit. Well, he just pissed me off, and I tore his ass up. And the promoter, right there, after the workout, says, "I'd like to have you February." This was like November. He said, "I'd like you to come over for the UWF in February."

JS: And the rest is history.

MF: Yeah. So I went over there, and Lou went with me. I got my ass kicked by Takada. First match.

JS: Yeah, but that was a work, right? Or no? Or was it all shoots?

MF: Well, it was a half-work, half-shoot. On your feet it was a shoot. On the mat it was a work.

JS: Okay.

MF: It pissed Lou off because, see, I was a mat wrestler.

JS: Right.

MF: Lou knew that. They acted like they didn't want to wrestle on the mat. They'd work on the mat and shoot on the feet. But, anyway, they were paying me well. Lou said, "You know, get the money, man. Get the money. That's what you're in this for." So I was getting paid well. They would invite people. You had to sign a contract every tour, and if they didn't want you, they wouldn't offer you a contract. I went over there 19 times for them.

JS: Wow. And that's when they bring in Danny Hodge and ...

MF: Yeah. Anybody that they used on their promotions were ex-shooters. They used the Iron Sheik. He was a shooter.

JS: From Iran, right?

MF: Yeah. Of course, he was old and beat up by then, but they brought him over. Gary Albright. Dan Severn. You know Dennis Kozlowski? He was a wrestler in the Olympics, a silver medalist. They brought him over.

JS: Robinson too, right?

MF: Billy Robinson. They brought him over to help train us. And Danny Hodge. Gosh, a lot of guys. We had to go to their dojo every day, man. They watched us like hawks. They kind of guarded us. We trained there five hours a day.

JS: And you did pretty well in their shoot promotions. It wasn't pure wrestling, right, because they had the kicking in it, too.

MF: And, see, that was new to me. I didn't know how to do that.

JS: Yeah, I'm the same way. That's a weird thing.

MF: I told Lou, "I just know how to wrestle." I said, "I don't know any of this." He said, "Go out there. Tumble with them. Tie them up and throw them off." He said, "Hurt the sons of bitches. Hurt them, man." So I'd just go out there, and I'd throw them, but those guys were good. They were smaller, but they were good.

JS: Tough guys.

MF: Yes, tough guys. They were very dedicated, very dedicated. And they would study pressure points and do all that stuff, but they were very sportsmanlike—you know what I'm saying?

JS: Polite and stuff.

MF: Very polite. They would try to kick your ass when you're out there. You had to fight for your life, but after it was over with, they shook your hand. They bowed to you. They didn't care. It was over with then.

JS: Yeah, yeah, Japanese culture is pretty cool.

MF: And the people over there liked the way I wrestled. I was pretty popular. And, of course, they announced me as Lou's protégé before every match. People liked that, of course. But if they liked you, they didn't just root for the Japanese. If you were good, like if I threw a jab, and it was a good suplex or a good belly-to-belly, man, they would stand up and clap. They didn't care if it was their guy. Now, if you did a cheap shot, like if you threw an elbow after the break, they wouldn't clap. They'd just be silent. They didn't go for that kind of stuff over there.

JS: It's a different kind of audience than the States.

MF: Oh, yeah. They're not bloodthirsty over there, like they are here. I mean, they want to see sport. They don't want to see bullshit.

JS: Yeah, it's a shame the way it's gone over here. I mean, let alone the cartoon circus that you see on TV, even with the shoot promotions here, you wrestle for a little bit, and then you get him on the ground and just beat him up.

MF: Yeah.

JS: There's not a lot of science in that. I mean, there's some submission, but most of that is the Brazilian jujitsu stuff.

MF: And this ultimate fighting stuff. You know what? I'm going to tell you this, me and Lou used to watch some of the tapes. Lou thought it was bullshit.

JS: Like works, some of them?

MF: I think he thought it was more bullshit than what he made everybody think.

JS: He liked Dan Severn a lot, huh?

MF: Oh, he liked Dan Severn, yeah. He thought Dan Severn was great. Dan Severn was a hell of a wrestler.

JS: Oh, yeah. He's got a great career.

MF: He's probably the best wrestler, I think, in my era, in my age group, best ever. He was the best. He could do it all. He could do Greco, he could do freestyle, he could do folkstyle, he could do submission style. Then he could do the street fighting. He could do it all. Of course, I can't say enough about him, but the guy, he's tops all the way. He's a professional. He's not cocky, not when I knew him. I just saw him a couple of years ago at the Wrestler Hall of Fame. He's a super guy, and Lou respected him, yeah.

JS: And you had some matches with Ken Shamrock, too, huh?

MF: I wrestled Ken Shamrock here, in the United States, only one time.

JS: But it was a work match, right?

MF: Yeah, well, when we were on the mat it wasn't. He and I really went at each other, but we were wrestling for a professional wrestling promotion. It was down in North Carolina. He was working there, I was working there, and they put us together. We went at it. Lou was in my corner, and Paul Jones was in his corner. It was a 30-minute draw on TV, and they showed the whole 30 minutes on the *TV Wrestling Show*.

JS: Wow.

MF: I thought that was pretty neat. And you know, he told me he had the tape. He was going to send it to me. He told me that at the airport in Japan—we saw each other. I haven't seen him since. He said he was going to send it to me, never did. But that was before he was a star. That was before he got into all this chute fighting stuff. But he's a heck of an athlete. I don't think he's the wrestler Dan Severn is—as a matter of fact, I know he's not—but he's tough, man, he's tough.

JS: And you toured a lot with Gary Albright, right?

MF: Oh, yeah, Gary Albright, golly. Man, he was there every time I was in Japan. As a matter of fact, for six months, over in Japan, he was ranked number one. Of course, Takada was the champion. He was ranked number one, and I was ranked number two, and I got knocked out by a guy that wasn't ranked. It knocked me out of the rankings over there. But Gary, Gary was a monster. Gary was scary. He was a Greco wrestler and tough as nails. He wasn't in the best of shape—as a matter of fact, he was in horrible shape. Never wanted to train. Never wanted to work out.

JS: Kind of like an Ed Lewis, huh?

MF: Worse. Gary, all he wanted to do was drink beer and fight. That's all he wanted to do.

JS: [*laughs*]

MF: But he was a hell of a wrestler, man. Greco. Just throwing you. He wasn't a technician. He'd just pick you up and throw you. The Japanese loved him. He and I were working out one day, at the dojo there, in Japan. I shot a single leg on him, and I yanked it, yanked it up, right, and popped it out. Popped the knee out of the socket.

JS: Oh Jesus.

MF: The damn Japanese were about to have a fit if they thought that he got hurt, and that damn Gary popped it right back in. He said, "Oh, shit." He said, "Oh, I'm all right. I'm all right." He told me the next day, "You son of a bitch [*laughing*]. You tried to hurt me." I said, "I didn't do it on purpose, man, hey. I just shot a single leg in on you. I don't know what happened." But they wanted him and me to wrestle. He was ranked number one. I was ranked number two, and they wanted him and me to wrestle in a main event in Yokohama, I think it was, and I had to sign the contract to come back to wrestle him.

We were sitting in a Hard Rock Cafe in Osaka, Japan, after the matches, and the promoter came up to me and Gary, and he said, "You two guys wrestle, number one and number two, wrestle next month at a main event." I said, "All right. That's cool." We were happy with it.

The promoter told me, "You take dive for Gary," and I said, "Oh." I didn't like the idea, but I said, "Okay," because I knew Gary could beat me in wrestling. You know what I'm saying?

JS: Yeah.

MF: So me and Gary and Lou, we were talking about it, and then the Japanese guy, the promoter, said, "Well, I'm going to tell you how it's going to end. It's going to end where he throws you in a full-up suplex."

Well, I wasn't too happy with that. Here I was, working my ass off for this promotion, had kicked everybody's ass over there that they had. They were building me up a little bit, and here he's going to beat me in such a dangerous fall. I said, "No way." And even Gary talked to him. He said, "Look. I don't need to beat Mark that way. That's a dangerous fall." I told him, "I'm not going down that way."

JS: Well, and you're a bigger guy, too, so to come down on your head like that could really cause some damage. Now, let me ask you this, we've covered your long journey through wrestling, from when you were 13 years old to being a ninth grader and getting on varsity and then state championships. Later, the Ricky Steamboat connection and then your getting to Japan and your connection with Lou. I know in the last couple of years you haven't done a lot, especially the work matches, and the bumps and stuff really take a toll on your body.

MF: Yeah, I'm pretty bad. I've got a bad back.

JS: Well, what do you see in terms of your future with wrestling? Do you see yourself coaching anybody, like, even kids?

MF: Well, around here, where I'm from, there's really no opportunity. Wrestling is really organized here. The coaches that are here are either teachers or PE teachers or something. In your school board, you have to be an employee of them to be a coach and get paid. I can be a volunteer. I've been doing it a long time, but I've got other things to do. You know what I'm saying?

JS: Right, right.

MF: But I thought about that one time. This old guy that used to wrestle with me in school—he's a referee for the amateurs around here—he tried to get me to referee. And I thought about it, and I almost did it, but then something told me not to do it, get involved in that, so I didn't do that. And after all this Japanese thing and Lou happened, my wife left me, and I kind of, believe it or not, I went through a—I hate to admit this—but I kind of went through a depression state. I was depressed. I really was. I didn't realize it at the time, but I realize it now. I was in a slump, man, I mean, I was bad off, and I missed wrestling. I thought my career was gone.

JS: And then you didn't have the tapes anymore or whatever?

MF: Yeah, I didn't have things. I don't know. A lot of things in my life changed. That was one year. I lost a grandfather. We were real close. A lot of things happened to me, and, believe it or not, it kicked my ass— I never really talked about it to anybody, never really admitted it—but it did, when I stop to think about it now. I guess everything happens for the better, but it was rough. It was quite rough.

JS: So, now I know that you and I have talked about maybe, someday, down the road, you'd like to get some sort of ring or something associated with your gym.

MF: Yeah, I just don't have the room. The gym that I've got now is more like a men and women's fitness center. I don't have the 2,600 square feet [242 m²].

JS: You'd like to throw a 12-by-12 [3.7 m by 3.7 m] ring or whatever.

MF: Right. I really don't have people coming in to ask. I just don't have the spot for it. And, to tell you the truth, I can't take the bumps now. I've got two herniated disks, and they want to operate on me.

JS: Oh.

MF: As a matter of fact, I wrestled three or four months ago, in a benefit here. I had to go get a physical to get my license renewed with the Athletic Commission. I went to the doctor to get my physical, and everything was fine, but he didn't want to give it to me because of my back.

JS: Wow.

MF: That's how bad my back is. I talked him into it. He was really reluctant to give me the physical because of my back. But anyway, I did that, and here I am now.

JS: So when you'd gone out [to Japan], and you'd worked with these guys, you'd leverage your strength, like tossing them around and stuff like that.

MF: Yup, yup.

JS: Take the fight out of them that way.

MF: Yup, yup. And they were just more technical than I was. I mean, I knew some stuff, but these guys, oh my gosh, they knew everything. They knew where to put the stop holds in. They'd get your pressure point. They knew all that stuff.

JS: Well, I told you that I had been talking with Karl Gotch, right? And he was telling me, "You know what? Of all the guys that I trained, Fujiwara was probably the best."

MF: I wrestled him. I wrestled Fujiwara.

JS: How'd that go?

MF: Tough as shit. Kicked my ass.

JS: Yeah.

MF: He head butted me and everything.

JS: No way, really?

MF: Oh, man, he'll head butt the shit out of you. When he's got you down, he'll start head butting you. And do you know, and this is another highlight—I don't know if I've ever told you this—after the matches, in the locker room—I was getting ready to get in the shower—he came in there, sat down, talked to me, and shook my hand, and told me how much he enjoyed our match. I thought that was pretty neat because he was a hard-nose over there. Yeah, you should see his notebook he carries around with him. He draws these wrestling moves and all this in his notebook. This guy is great, man, and he's not big. He's got little pencil arms. He's not big at all, not built at all, but tough as shit and knows how to wrestle.

JS: That's awesome.

MF: But, man, he got me down. He was head butting me and everything. He was tough.

Mark Fleming is a very humble, sincere and straight-forward person and many consider him Lou Thesz's true protégé. He currently runs his own fitness gym in Virginia Beach, Fleming's Gym.

★ ★ ★ PART 3 ★ ★ ★
TECHNIQUES

"At first, although enormously strong, my strength was of little avail, and a good wrestler would be sure to throw me, but later, when I understood the science of wrestling, I became invulnerable to the attacks of the best wrestlers that could be found to compete with me; and after this date, I was never defeated, either in wrestling or weight-lifting."
—Arthur Saxon in *The Development of Physical Power*[20]

ARE GREAT CATCH WRESTLERS BORN OR MADE?

The study of excellence, whether in sport, art, or science, has long been an area of intense scrutiny and debate. However, Adriann de Groot—in *Thought and Choice in Chess*, his seminal work on chess experts—was the first to systematically apply the scientific method to the study of

---

20 Arthur Saxon, *The Development of Physical Power* (New York: Healtheaux Publishing Co., 1931), 10.

human expertise.[21] The study of the acquisition of expert performance matured into its own full-fledged interdisciplinary research program with economist Herbert A. Simon's work. He is one of the principal founders of artificial intelligence, a leading researcher and modeler of human cognition, and the winner of the 1978 Nobel Prize in Economic Sciences. Simon coined a psychological law, called the 10-Year Rule, that recognizes that it takes approximately a decade of serious effort to master any field.[22] Later studies have shown that this holds true in other areas of excellence, including sports.[23] Recent cognitive science research shows that a strong motivation to excel is far more important than innate talent when it comes to making an expert. This type of motivation drives the deliberate practice that creates masters. As Aristotle said, "Repetition is the mother of skill."

WHAT IS DELIBERATE PRACTICE?

Leading expertise theorist K. Anders Ericsson of Florida State University argues that, while experience is important, deliberate practice, or "effortful study," is crucial to mastering any subject. Effortful study means to constantly tackle the challenges that lie just beyond your skill set. Deliberate practice is the difference between the enthusiast who never advances beyond the basics despite hours of practice (of grappling, chess, a foreign language, or any other discipline) and the properly trained individual who eclipses others relatively quickly.

What separates deliberate practice from non-deliberate practice is the concentration required to move from being competent at a skill to

---

21 Presented in Adriaan de Groot, *Thought and Choice in Chess* (New York: Mouton Publishers, 1978).

22 Herbert A. Simon puts forth his findings in "Skill in Chess," *American Scientist*, Issue 61 (1973): 394–403.

23 For more on the subject, see Dr. Benjamin Bloom, *Developing Talent in Young People* (New York: Ballantine Books, 1985).

mastering it. Repetitive performance, critical analysis, and feedback-based improvements transform practitioners into masters. The authors of "Deliberate Practice in Sports: What Is It Anyway?"[24] studied the practice activities of skilled figure skaters and competitive wrestlers. Club and international wrestlers, including retired wrestlers, were polled and asked to share the statistics from their training journals.

The wrestlers seemed to engage in non-wrestling activities to maintain conditioning (mostly solo activities, such as swimming, cycling, running, weights, diet planning, watching wrestling, and mental rehearsal, but also team activities like coaching, sparring, and drilling). The authors dug into the microstructure of practice using univariate and multivariate analysis of variance (ANOVA and MANOVA) to determine the difference between the hours spent in practice of club-level wrestlers and of international-level wrestlers.

There was no significant difference between the two groups in time spent practicing solo activities. However, when it came to team practice, international athletes put in, on average, one extra hour of training each week compared to club-level athletes. International athletes were also more consistent in their practice. As expected, the international athletes put in more deliberate practice time. Also, the skill level of the teams at the international level may have a significant impact on the team members, pushing them to higher levels of performance and learning. According to the wrestlers' ratings in this study, the most relevant practice behavior is the time spent on the mat working with another wrestler, and the time spent working with a coach was a close second.

What this means for the aspiring wrestler is that not only do you have to put in the time at team practice, but you also need to practice with people who are better than you.

---

24 Janet L. Starkes and Nicola J. Hodges at McMaster University in Hamilton, Ontario, came together with Janice M. Deakin and April Hayes at Queen's University, Kingston, Ontario, and Fran Allard at the University of Waterloo, Waterloo, Ontario to author "Deliberate Practice in Sports: What Is It Anyway?," a chapter in *The Road to Excellence: The Acquisition of Expert Performance in the Arts and Sciences, Sports and Games*, ed. K. Anders Ericsson (Mahwah, NJ: Lawrence Erlbaum Associates, 1996).

The idea of deliberate practice is covered in the first book of Martin "Farmer" Burns's classic *Lessons in Wrestling and Physical Culture*. Also, there has been a lot of talk of athletes in various sports "being in the zone" or attaining "flow" since Mihaly Csikszentmihalyi's 1990 book *Flow: The Psychology of Optimal Performance*. The flow state, as commonly understood, represents a state of pleasure, well-being, or euphoria that occurs when you are performing a task at a level with a perfect match between demand and skill. What this means for the wrestler is that you should push yourself just beyond the "zone" or "flow" state—into effortful study— during your club practices. You can thereby achieve a perfect match between demand and skill during competitions.

> The science of scientific wrestling is so deep that it cannot be learned in a few days or a few months, but as you continue the wrestling year after year, you will constantly add to your knowledge and skill until you become a real master of the fine points of the profession.
>
> Use your head fully as much as you do your muscle. Think and plan and scheme constantly while practicing and then when you will get into real contests you will have formed the habit of good generalship.
>
> —"Farmer" Burns in his *Lessons in Wrestling and Physical Culture*, Book X[25]

PHYSICAL PRINCIPLES

Since grappling is often likened to a game of physical chess, it is appropriate that we begin our investigation of the principles of catch-as-catch-can with a look at the mental combat in chess. During his 1946 study of expert- and grandmaster-level chess performances, de Groot

---

25   http://www.sandowplus.co.uk/Competition/Burns/lessons/lesson10.htm

discovered that, contrary to popular belief, the most skilled players did not actually think moves ahead (that is, use "search algorithms"). Instead, the evidence revealed that skilled players' superior performances were based on knowledge and principles.

Follow-up research by Simon and Chase suggested that "chunks" of memory (that is, conceptual patterns or "principles") rather than superior IQ or innate talent allowed experts to outperform novices when both were exposed to identical structured chess positions. Likewise, in physics, it has been observed that the representation of an expert physicist's domain is a "principled" one, whereas the novice's representations are more situational.[26]

Practicing the following three principles will help a novice catch wrestler master the sport.

PRINCIPLE #1: SCIENTIFIC METHOD/GAMENESS

Unless you are willing to test it on the mat, you should not call yourself a wrestler.

Generally, the "scientific method" refers to the techniques used to investigate claims and to acquire reliable knowledge. These techniques are informed by observable, empirical, and quantifiable evidence that is subject to critical review and logical reasoning.

The concepts of "testing" and "proof" are paramount in science. In this vein, every catch wrestling match can be loosely considered an experiment performed on the wrestling mat. As such, proof of skill is paramount, and the phrase "put up or shut up" harkens back to the original professional Lancashire-style bouts of the post–American Civil War period and late 19th century, when each fighter would bring a matching purse and the winner would take all. This willingness to put their own money on the line provided all fighters with unparalleled incentive to hard work and also prevented collusion between fighters.

---

26 M.T.H. Chi, P. Feltovich, and R. Glaser, "Categorization and Representation of Physics Problems by Experts and Novices," *Cognitive Science 5* (1981): 121–152.

This created the rigorous environment needed for the testing and refining of the techniques and strategies of catch wrestling.

PRINCIPLE #2: BIO-MECHANICAL ADVANTAGE

Understanding mechanical advantage allows the catch-as-catch-can practitioner to successfully adapt and improvise against a wide array of opponents.

Catch wrestlers must implicitly understand the principles of mechanical advantage as they apply to the human anatomy. In physics and engineering, mechanical advantage is the number of times a simple machine multiplies your effort or force. Simple machines fall into two general camps: those that are dependent on the vector resolution of forces (the inclined plane, wedge, and screw) and those in which there is an equilibrium of torques (the lever, pulley, and wheel). A catch wrestler applies simple machines to the human anatomy. In any catch wrestling match, the concepts of the wheel, axle, lever, and pulley are employed in an attempt to pin or submit an opponent. Successful submissions are very much rooted in the principles of classical mechanics.

For example, the crooked head scissor uses the torque of the wheel (on the head) and axel (on the neck) to generate damaging force to the neck; the straight arm bar uses the lever and fulcrum to damage the elbow joint; and the flying mare uses your opponent's arm as the lever and your own body as the fulcrum (the axis of rotation). In catch wrestling, you must impose your will upon your opponent while obeying not just the rules of catch wrestling but the rules of physics, too.

Some examples of how the rules of physics apply to wrestling follow.

STABILITY: The stronger your base of support is, the greater your stability will be. Offensively, you seek to destroy your opponent's stability while optimizing your own (for example, when you break down your opponent to the mat). Defensively, you seek to maintain stability despite your opponent's intentions otherwise (for example, the sprawl).

FORCE: It changes the inertia (resting or moving) of an object. It is important to know

★ magnitude (i.e., how much?),

★ line of action (i.e., direction: horizontal, vertical, in between?), and

★ point of application (i.e., where?).

INERTIA: It allows a body to continue doing what it is doing. Any change is directly proportionate to the amount of force applied on it.

★ Newton's first law: A body at rest tends to stay at rest; a body in motion tends to stay in motion.

★ Newton's second law: The rate of change in the momentum of an object is directly proportional to the amount of force exerted upon the object.

★ Momentum: The product of mass and velocity.

WORK: It is the product of force and distance. Newton's third law (the law of reciprocal actions) states that objects in contact exert equal and opposite force on each other.

LEVER: In the human body, bones represent bars, joints represent fulcrums, and muscle contractions represent force.

★ First-class lever (or fulcrum): Like a standard seesaw (a plank with a fulcrum), the human head balances on the fulcrum of the neck portion of the spine—and this is just one example of a fulcrum in the human body. First-class levers do not produce a great deal of force, and, therefore, areas of the body that employ first-class levers are a favored point of attack for the catch wrestler.

★ Second-class lever (or load): The object to be moved is placed between the axis of rotation and the point of application of force. For example, the forearm is employed as the "load arm" for a sleeper choke.

★   Third-class lever (or effort): This is the most common type of lever in the human body. It is the least energy efficient of the three levers because the input effort is higher than the output load (however, the input effort travels a shorter distance than the output load, hence an advantage is still gained from a third-class lever). The human arm is a perfect example. A catch wrestler will seek to exploit the energy differential between the input effort and the output load by grasping the arm at the point furthest from its fulcrum (by applying pressure to the elbow joint, for example).

PULLEY: It is a wheel with a grooved rim through which a cord passes. A pulley changes the direction of the force applied to the cord and is typically used to raise heavy weights. In the human body, the quadriceps tendon acts like a cord as it goes over the patella (the wheel) and into the tibia bone in the shin (the weight). The catch wrestler is mostly interested in how to damage a pulley system, either through a twisting, torque motion (as in the heel hook which twists the knee) or through the use of a wedge (as in the short-arm scissor which uses a wedge to separate the elbow joint).

TORQUE: It's the magnitude of a twist (rotary movement) around an axis of rotation (fulcrum).

GRAVITY: Gravity and the ground are weapons for the catch wrestler.
★   Center of gravity: It's the point in the human body around which weight is evenly distributed.
★   Line of gravity: A vertical line that runs straight down the body from the center of gravity. If a wrestler's line of gravity falls outside his base of support he will either be in motion or falling.

APPLIED BIOMECHANICAL ADVANTAGE AND SUBMISSION GRAPPLING

Joint/Process	Type	Submission	Simple Machine
Spine	Trochoidal	Wrestler's guillotine / crooked head scissor	Wheel (torque)
		Boston crab	Fulcrum (first-class lever)
Shoulder	Enarthrodial	Telephone TWL	Wheel (torque)
		Key lock	
Elbow	Ginglymus	Short arm scissor	Wedge
		Arm bar	Fulcrum (first-class lever)
Knee		Heel hook	Wheel (torque)
		Leg bar	Fulcrum (first-class lever)
Ankle and foot	Arthrodial	Toehold	Wheel (torque) and fulcrum (first-class lever)
		Achilles lock	Fulcrum (first-class lever)
Breathing	Cardiovascular	Sleeper	Load (second-class lever)
		Front cravat	Fulcrum (first-class lever)

"Wrestling is the opposite of what most people think it is; it is not strength but knowledge, balance, and timing that win in the noble art of wrestling."—Karl Gotch

PRINCIPLE #3: CONDITIONING AND WEARING OUT YOUR OPPONENT

"Conditioning is your greatest hold."—Karl Gotch

Catch wrestling is a physical endeavor, and catch wrestlers must possess exceptional physical conditioning in order to actively wrestle under catch rules. Physical conditioning not only helps prevent serious in-jury, it helps ensure a win when two wrestlers of equal weight and skill meet.

A by-product of superior physical conditioning is the ability to wear down your opponent, both physically and mentally. The catch wrestler seeks to create panic—a sensation of drowning or reactive fear—in his opponent while remaining as calm, relaxed, and rational as possible. The catch wrestler can thereby influence both his own nervous system and that of his opponent, maximizing his chances of winning. While the catch wrestler seeks to stimulate his opponent's nervous system—so it releases epinephrine, the hormone produced by the adre-nal gland that causes the "fight or flight" response—through aggressive and painful offensive maneuvers, he strives to control his own nervous system by remaining calm. He conditions himself to withstand the pain and strain of grappling through consistent and deliberate practice, which drives the necessary neural adaptations. These neural adapta-tions lead to the qualities of "mental toughness" and being "in the zone" found in all high-level athletes.

In Book x of his *Lessons in Wrestling and Physical Culture*, "Farmer" Burns states,

> Here are two things to always keep in mind.
> First: Save your own strength.
> Second: Make your opponent waste his strength.
>
> You save your own strength by resting your body or parts of your body whenever possible. A rest of only a few seconds for an arm or leg will sometimes do a tremendous good.
>
> One of the most effective ways to wear your opponent out is to compel him to carry your weight as much as pos-sible. When standing on your feet or on the mat, throw your weight on his neck and shoulders dozens of times, in fact, whenever you can. Also, when working on the mat, follow the same practice. Drop your full weight on his back,

head, or shoulders many, many times, and the effect after
15 or 20 minutes will really be wonderful.[27]

THE USE OF INDIAN CLUBS AND MACES

The Indian club was monumentally popular in the West as recently as
the early 20th century. Indian clubs were first featured in the 1904
Olympics in St. Louis, under the category of rhythmic gymnastics, and
remained an Olympic sport until 1932. Indian club swinging is now
making a comeback and gaining popularity.

They originated in ancient Persia, where they were known as *meels*.
These *meels* were used by the Pahlavan (Persian grapplers and strong-
men) to increase their strength, endurance, and health. The lighter version
generally weighed 10 to 15 pounds (5–7 kg) and was used in high-rep
sets to build stamina, while the heavier class weighed 25 to 60 pounds
(11–27 kg) and was used to build strength. According to longtime
Pahlavani researcher Farzad Nekoogar, Persian grapplers first brought
meels to India in the 13th century. Indian club swinging is likely a deriva-
tive of the ancient war club or mace. In India the mace is called the
gada, and it is a powerful symbol of keen physical prowess and moun-
tainous strength. Many depictions of the Hindu gods and goddesses in
religious art show the deity brandishing a war club of some kind.

Probably the most famous and most feared embodiment of the
club-swinging athlete was a man known as the Lion of the Punjab, the
Great Gama Baksh. He was born into a famous family of grapplers
from the northwestern part of India. To give you the scope of his com-
manding physical presence, Gama had 30-inch (76-cm) thighs and a
56-inch (142-cm) chest. His daily exercise routine is said to have included 3,000 *bethaks* (free squats), 1,500 *dands* (jackknifing push-ups),
and a one-mile (1.6-km) run with a 120-pound (54-kg) stone ring

---

27 http://www.sandowplus.co.uk/Competition/Burns/lessons/lesson10.htm

around his neck. In 1908, two years before he went to London to compete for the world championship belt, Gama's regimen was increased to 5,000 *bethaks* and 3,000 *dands*. Every morning he would also work out by wrestling with 40 compatriot wrestlers in the royal court. He also began weight lifting with a 100-pound (45-kg) grindstone and a *santola* (a wooden barbell made from a tree trunk). His phenomenal diet and exercise regimen were meant to develop a pervasive and subtle energy rather than just the kinetic power of particular muscle groups. Even at the age of 50, Gama was still doing 6,000 *bethaks* and 4,000 *dands* every day and wrestling with 80 compatriots in the royal court.

Clearly Gama's regimen encompassed much more than just the Indian club; nonetheless, it's a big part of every Indian wrestler's training. While stationed in India during the 19th century, the British army used Indian club exercises as part of its own military physical training (PT) regimen. In 1861, an American fitness enthusiast and businessman by the name of Sim D. Kehoe observed the art of Indian club swinging while visiting England. Soon thereafter, in 1862, he began to produce and sell clubs on the American market.

Today, there is a resurgence of interest in Indian clubs among modern physical culturists, especially combat athletes. The club's non-linear motions work the shoulder girdle and core like nothing else. Mace-work also improves your grip. If you are interested in changing up your routine and challenging yourself with the Macebell, it is a brutal strength-training implement that will earn your respect.[28]

CLIMBING DOWN THE MOUNTAIN

How many of us have set a goal to complete 500 Hindu squats only to fall short? Karl Gotch's criterion for showing a wrester anything he

---

28 Vincent Giordano has made a DVD, *The Physical Body: Indian Wrestling and Physical Culture*, with tons of footage of authentic Indian club swinging in all its variations. It was filmed on location in the wrestling pits of India.

knew was that the wrestler had to perform 500 Hindu squats, 250
Hindu push-ups, and hold a three-minute bridge. "Climbing Down the
Mountain" is a method I've developed that has helped others meet this
target. If you can do 100 Hindu squats and 50 Hindu push-ups without
stopping, you should be able to get to 500 and 250, respectively, in a
couple of days—though you will be sore on your first try. For you to
meet your target of 500 Hindu squats, this is how your sets for squats
should proceed:

100 squats

rest

90 squats

rest

80 squats

rest

70 squats

rest

60 squats

rest

40 squats (a jump to keep us at a total of 500 squats)

rest

30 squats

rest

20 squats

rest

10 squats

Voilà! You just did 500 squats! As you get better and better, shrink the
rest periods toward zero, and you will soon be doing 500 continuous
Hindu squats.

This method can be applied to any body-weight exercise, allowing you to increase the total number of reps you complete in any one set
amazingly quickly. I've applied this same formula to Hindu push-ups

and pull-ups with similar success. Simply find your maximum number of reps for one set and climb down the mountain. Each week, test your one-set max reps (the number should increase) and climb down from there. That math class in high school actually had some sort of real-world value after all!

"BUDDY" WEIGHT CONDITIONING

Buddy lifts is a strength-training method rather unknown outside of wrestling rooms. The only equipment you really need for buddy lifts is a friend—preferably someone who weighs roughly the same as you or less, especially if you happen to be a beginner to strength training. Regardless of whether you can dead lift or back-squat twice your body weight, you will want to start with a lighter buddy because a "live" weight can be awkward.

Live weight actively recruits compensatory and stabilization muscles in a way that "dead" weight does not. You'll want to be careful with these oft-underused stabilizers until you are familiar with lifting live weight. Though there is much here with which an experienced weight lifter will be familiar, lifting with a live weight must be felt to be truly understood.

Here are some basic guidelines for lifting "live" weight to avoid injury to yourself or your buddy:

★ If you can't carry their weight, then don't lift them. Take care of your partner! They trust you, and they should have every reason to do so.

★ Use proper form. If you have any question about how to perform the lift, ask a qualified coach first.

★ Put some "oomph" into it. Once you are confident that you have proper form and you can protect your partner, lift ballistically. This means to lift as explosively and powerfully as you safely can.

★ Never, ever use children or animals for your buddy lifts. Even if they have soiled your favorite pair of shoes or ruined an expensive piece of furniture, they are off-limits for this activity. Only use partners who can make fully informed decisions regarding their participation and welfare.

★ Do not lift while ill or injured; you'll only make things worse.
★ Only lift if you can maintain perfect form. Once your form degrades due to fatigue or an overly heavy load, immediately stop and call it a day.

Buddy lifting exercises can be split into basic, intermediate, and advanced exercises depending on their level of complexity.

THE BASICS: START HERE

These exercises are a great way to begin your training in partner-resistance exercises.

LEG PUSHING

Have your partner lie down on his back. Step around so that you are standing over him with one foot on each side of his head. His left hand grabs your left ankle, and his right hand grabs your right ankle.

Your partner then raises his legs (so his posture is L-shaped), and you push his feet forward hard and toward the ground. He resists and tries not to let his feet hit the ground. He then brings his legs up again, and you push them back to the ground.

Beginners can start with 15 repetitions and work their way up to 50 repetitions per set.

PIGGYBACK RIDE

Most people should be familiar with this activity, even if they haven't done it since childhood. Once your partner jumps on your back you have three basic options—walk for distance, perform lunges, or perform squats.

TAKING OUT THE TRASH

After assuring your partner that the name of this exercise in no way reflects your personal estimation of his character, grab him from behind in a bear hug around the waist (both of you should be facing the same direction now).

Walk a distance of, say, a little over 300 feet (100 m) forward, and then switch positions and have your partner carry you back.

This lift can be performed with the lifter walking both forward and backward (just make sure you have a clear path to avoid stumbling).

HONEYMOONS

Think of the classic image of a groom carrying his bride across the threshold. Lift your partner like this, and then walk for distance, perform lunges, or perform squats.

INTERMEDIATE PARTNER LIFTS

Once you feel comfortable with carrying live weight, you can add these lifts into the mix.

SINGLE LEG LIFT

Stand at your partner's side, squat down, and hug your partner's leg with a classic dead-lift posture (your hips underneath you and your head up). For the most efficient grip, make sure both of your palms are facing up and are one on top of the other. This grip is similar to doing a bicep curl with your hands together when done correctly. From there, stand up straight, lifting your partner into the air and slightly load his weight onto your chest by putting your hips firmly beneath you. This exercise can be done for reps or you can walk for distance.

WHEELBARROW

Another long-forgotten gem from childhood, this one is performed by walking on your hands while your partner holds your feet. To make it challenging, do a push-up between every step or try doing this exercise up and down a flight of stairs. It ain't rocket science, but it will definitely challenge you and put some fun back into your workout!

BACKWARD SADDLE SIT-UP

It sounds complicated, but it really isn't. Your partner gets down on all fours. You sit down on his back, but instead of facing forward, like riding a horse, you face the other direction (toward your partner's feet).

Once you are comfortable, hook your legs into his legs, so that when you lean back to do the sit-up you are stabilized. Cross your arms across your chest and lean back as far as you can. As you do, your partner should begin to feel the load increase on his neck and shoulders. This way, while you are working your abdominal muscle, your partner is also working hard.

Do as many sit-ups as you can until you can reach 50 repetitions without trouble.

MORE ADVANCED BUDDY LIFTS

These progressions are a little more complicated, and you should only practice them after you have mastered the basic and intermediate buddy lifts.

DEAD-MAN LIFT

Stand directly above your partner as he lies face down. With one foot on each side of him, reach under his belly and clasp your hands. Assume a classic dead-lift posture, with your head up and your hips underneath you.

Lift your partner with your legs, swinging him forward as you stand upright. Repeat from the beginning position with your partner lying completely flat.

FIREMAN'S CARRY

Face your partner. Pull your partner onto your shoulders by grabbing his same-side bicep (for example, your left hand grabs his right bicep). Next, duck your head underneath that same side armpit (following the above example, his right armpit).

Bend down slightly while maintaining a good load-bearing posture (head up and hips squarely underneath you), and grab your partner's leg with your other arm (to continue with the earlier example, your right arm hugs his right leg). Pull your partner completely onto your shoulders and stand up completely.

From there, you can walk for distance or perform squats and/or lunges.

SQUAD PUSH-UP

This is for when you have more than one partner to work out with. All participants assume push-up position in a circle. Place your feet on the shoulders of the person on your left. Be sure to place the shoelaces portion of your feet, not your tiptoes, on your neighbor's back. The person to the right of you will place his feet on your shoulders, creating an unbroken human chain when done correctly. Once in position, everyone will do push-ups in unison until the weakest link in the chain cannot continue.

REVERSE LIFT

This is a classic lift from Greco-Roman wrestling. Have your partner lie flat on his stomach and kneel to one side of him. Wrap your arms around his waist and clasp your hands together underneath his body.

Be certain that, when you grasp your partner, your arm that is on the same side as his feet reaches under his near side and your arm that is on the same side as his head and arms reaches around the far side of his body. With your arms clasped thus and from your kneeling position, pull your partner up and onto your lap. Now get to one knee and then to both feet.

Here's the tricky part: swing your partner's legs to the other side of your body. To do so, stand tall, and, giving a slight pop with your hips, pull with your clasped arms.

Lower your partner all the way to the ground so that he is flat again, and then repeat the lift.

PARTNER PLYOMETRICS

Make sure you are fresh when attempting these so you don't jump on top of your partner. Have your partner lie face down, and then stand to one side of his body. Next, simply jump back and forth over his body. Work up to 50 jumps per set.

For a more advanced workout, have your partner get on all fours and jump over the higher obstacle that they now present.

THE FLIP OVER

Your partner gets down on all fours. You go to one side of him and reach underneath him with both of your arms, grabbing his ribs at the far side. Now place your chin on his back, on the far side of his body.

Once you are in position and are securely holding your partner, kick both of your legs completely over his body while holding tight. When done properly, you will end up on the other side of your partner, with your belly to the ceiling and your head underneath his ribcage.

From there, kick back over your partner, back to your original position. Flip over your partner like this as many times as you safely can.

TECHNIQUES

There are three main types of positions: standing, on top, and underneath.

STANDING CATCH-AS-CATCH-CAN

STANCE

Head up, elbows in, shoulders in upright stance, and weight evenly distributed over the balls of the feet.

THE PIVOT

Mastering the pivot is crucial for your standing game. From your beginning stance, step forward and aim your lead foot in the direction you will be turning. Shift the weight of your lead foot and sweep your rear leg around, turning your body 180 degrees.

THROWING WITH A PIVOT

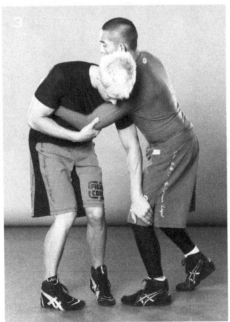

From the over/under tie-up, shift your opponent's weight over his lead leg. Holding your opponent's elbow securely, step and pivot. As you finish your 180-degree rotation, block the opponent's knee and take him down.

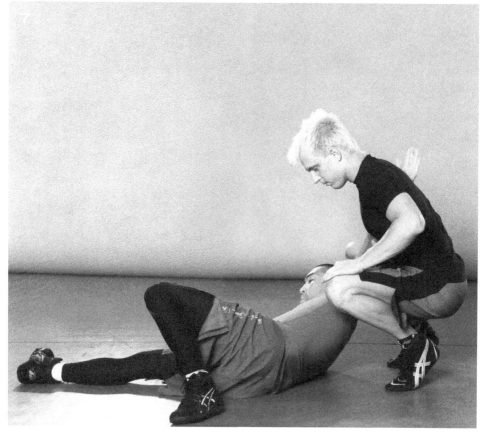

MARE

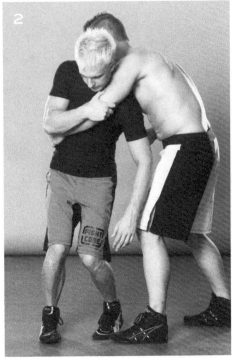

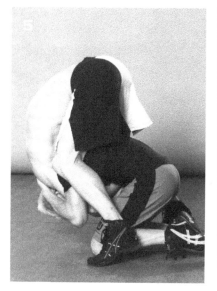

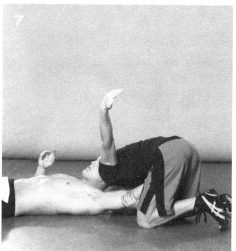

From the over/under tie-up position, slip your under arm free while stepping and pivoting with your same-side arm. With your free arm, scoop under your opponent's arm and grab his deltoid firmly as you finish your 180-degree pivot. Drop back onto your knees while holding your opponent's arm fast, taking him over. While maintaining a hold on your opponent's elbow, swim your other arm up and over his body to secure him for the pin.

ARM DRAG TO RUN-THE-PIPE TO STANDING ACHILLES

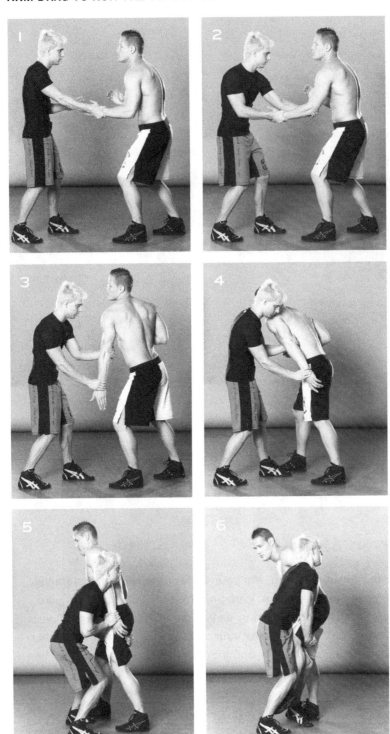

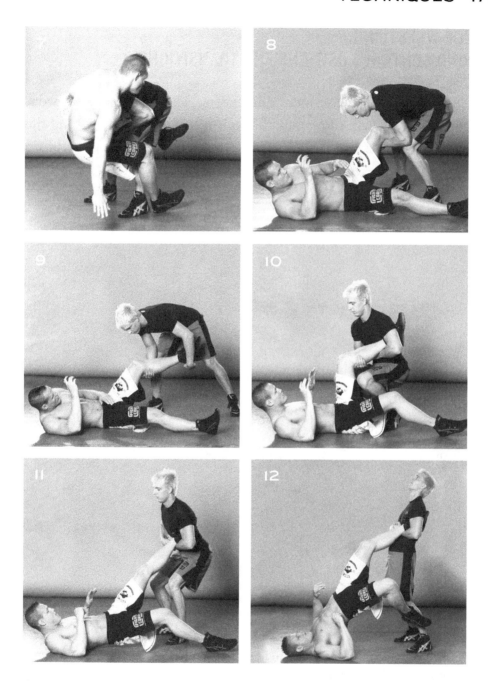

Grab your opponent's same-side wrist with one hand and secure his elbow with the other, and then hyperextend his elbow and lever him toward you. When he comes close to you, to relieve the pressure, grab his leg securely. Step and pivot while bowing to take him down. Step back outside his leg and over-hook your opponent's leg while placing the cutting blade of your wrist against his Achilles tendon. Stand and arch in a balanced manner to apply pressure.

ON-TOP WRESTLING:
GROUND CONTROL POSITIONS AND TRANSITIONS

Note: These positions are mere guideposts. Think of them as peda-gogical devices to help those new to catch-as-catch-can understand the basic building blocks of this amazing grappling style. They are in no way meant to represent an exhaustive list of positions and transitions.

TOP POSITION ONE—HEAD AND ARM

Notice the strong angles created by the top man's physiology. His legs and arms form approximate 90-degree angles. All the weight is on the man, not the mat. What you may not be able to see is that the only portion of the top man's body that is touching the mat is his toes (even his hips are slightly off the mat so the bottom man bears all of the top man's weight).

TOP POSITION TWO—FRONT NORTH/SOUTH

Again, all the weight is on the man, not the mat. The bottom man is carrying all of the top man's weight, and the only part of the top man's body that is touching the mat is his toes. The top man's elbows should be digging into the bottom man's armpits for control. The top man is focusing on driving his weight through his hipbone so he can pin the bottom man's face with it.

TOP POSITION THREE—FRONT CROSS BODY

As the top man maneuvers, he maintains pressure on the defensive man underneath.

TOP POSITION FOUR—FRONT LEG RIDE

The top man transitions to a top leg ride by resting both of his shins across the bottom man's quadriceps/hips. This gives the top man mobility, so he can shift around freely.

TOP POSITION FIVE—SATURDAY NIGHT RIDE

For the catch-as-catch-can wrestler, this position is a great place to enter into leg locks. If the bottom man is a Brazilian jujitsu player, he may offer offense from the bottom position (which they call "the guard"). As such, the top man should be wary of chokes and arm attacks from the bottom man.

TOP POSITION SIX—REAR CROSS BODY WITH CROSS FACE

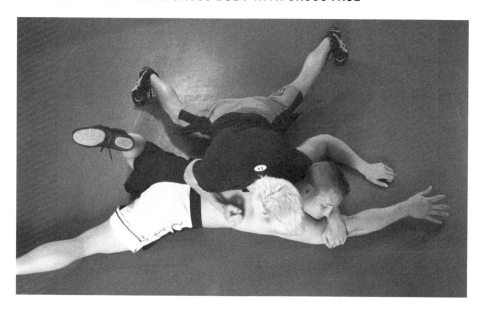

The cross face is an excellent way to control an opponent and is unusually uncomfortable for him.

TOP POSITION SEVEN—REAR NORTH/SOUTH

The rear north/south position differs from the top variation in that the bottom man's skull is firmly in the concave area created under the top man's rib cage.

TOP POSITION EIGHT—REAR LEG RIDE

This position is similar to the top leg ride position, the primary difference being that the bottom man is face down.

TOP POSITION NINE—BALL-AND-CHAIN RIDE

The top man scoops and compresses his opponent's ankle between his hamstring and calf. Securing his opponent's hip offers the top wrestler a great amount of control.

TOP POSITION TEN—SIDE RIDE

The top man grapevines one leg in and hooks the bottom man's leg while distributing his weight evenly across his opponent's hips.

TRANSITION FROM HEAD AND ARM TO CROSS BODY TO FRONT NORTH/SOUTH

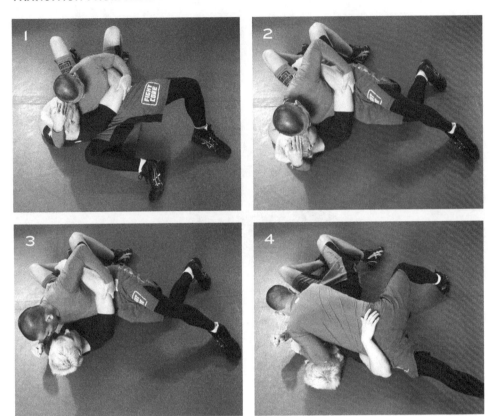

Take note, the top man maintains control throughout the position change. As he moves, the top man slips his right arm from controlling the head to pinning the bottom man's left bicep. Before removing his right pinning arm, the top man pins his opponent's face with his left arm, eventually replacing his left arm with his left hip bone. This frees both arms for offense while maintaining the top (i.e., dominant) position.

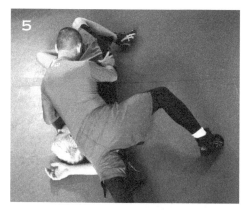

TRANSITION FROM FRONT NORTH/SOUTH TO TOP LEG RIDE

From the front north/south position, the top man controls the bottom man as he spins about 180 degrees. The top man's weight is on the man, not the mat, as only his toes are on the mat.

TRANSITION FROM SATURDAY NIGHT RIDE TO REAR CROSS BODY WITH CROSS FACE

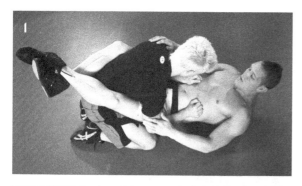

(continued on next page)

Keeping his weight over his legs and hips, the top man breaks the bottom man's leg scissor and under-hooks the bottom man's knee with his same-side arm. Keeping pressure on the bottom man with his shoulder, the top man torques the bottom man over, into a belly-down position (using the bottom man's bent leg like an Allen wrench). The top man slides up his opponent's body, keeping his opponent's leg bent with his body weight until he can slap on the cross face and finish in the cross-body position.

(Transition from Saturday night ride to rear cross body with cross face continued.)

(Transition from Saturday night ride to rear cross body with cross face continued.)

TRANSITION FROM REAR NORTH/SOUTH TO REAR LEG RIDE TO BALL-AND-CHAIN RIDE

The top man maintains weight on his opponent while spinning 180 degrees from rear north/south into the rear leg ride position. The top man moves his weight back, so the bottom man will begin to push up into a high defensive position. Meanwhile, the top man slides off to one side of the bottom man, pivoting on his knee and scooping his opponent's ankle between his calf and hamstring. The top man then sits down, trapping his opponent's leg and securing the leg with his arm. With his other arm, he grabs his opponent's toes and applies the toehold submission.

UNDERNEATH POSITIONS

LOW DEFENSIVE POSITION

HIGH DEFENSIVE POSITION

TRANSITION FROM SHORT SIT-OUT TO ARM ROLL

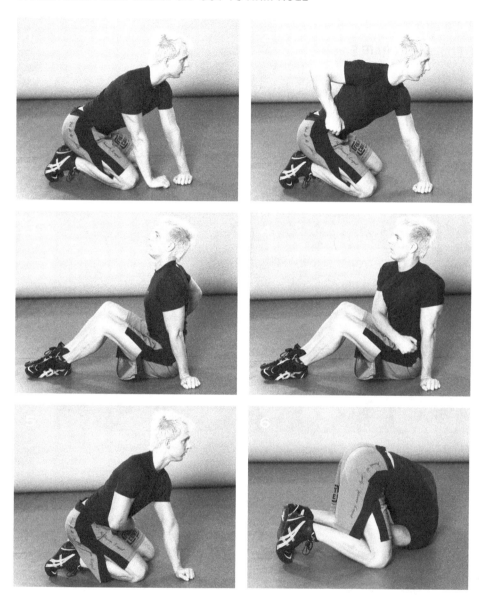

A drilling move that takes an opponent over from an underneath position. The bottom man pivots with his arm while securing the top man's wrist at the hip (only the bottom man is pictured here so that his movements are clear). Posting on the pivot arm, the bottom man performs a short sit-out by turning 180-degrees (notice the strong, upright posture). The bottom man takes the slack out of his opponent's arm by pulling it tight across to the opposite hip. Maintaining the tight hold on his opponent's arm, the bottom man rotates back to his original position then takes the top man over by bringing his shoulder to the mat.

SUBMISSIONS AND PINS

THE FUJIWARA CRADLE

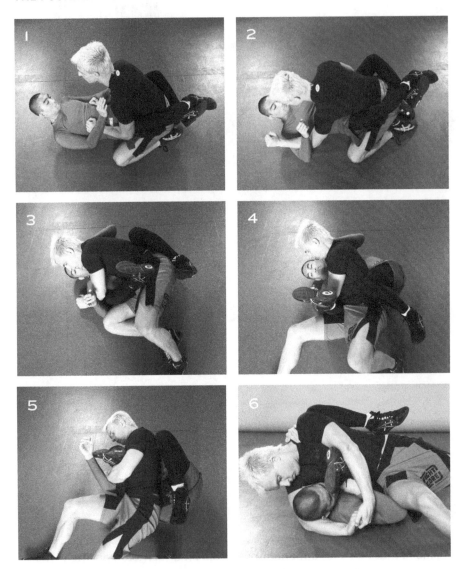

Yoshiaki Fujiwara showed this maneuver to me in 2006. While in the Saturday night ride position, begin posting your weight onto the bottom man's extremities, first with your forearm on his biceps, then by sitting out and pinning his leg. With your other hand, cradle your opponent's head. Grasp the bottom man's lat/armpit firmly so he doesn't pop his head out and take your back. Once secure, scoop your opponent's ankle into the crux of your elbow and begin to walk his toes toward his nose.

GAG FROM REAR NORTH/SOUTH

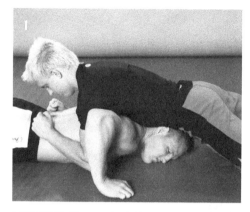 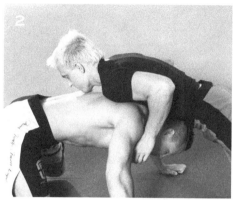

 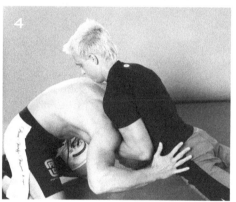

When the bottom man begins to push up into a high defensive position, simply cup his chin with both hands. Once your hands are in place, drive forward with your hips while pulling your cupped hands toward yourself, thereby compressing your opponent's trachea.

SHOULDER LOCK/TELEPHONE LOCK SUBMISSION COMBINATION FROM HEAD AND ARM POSITION

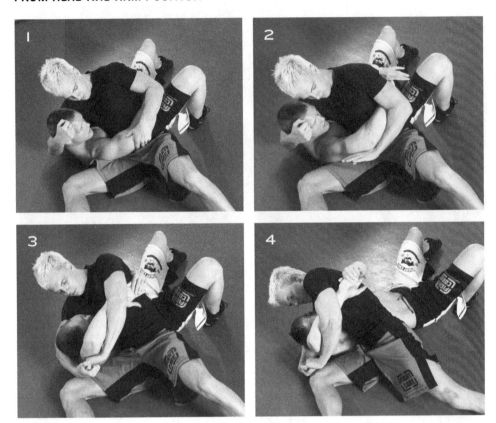

Slide the cutting bone of your wrist underneath your opponent's elbow, and then clasp your hands together and crush his elbow or shoulder to his head with your arms and weight. If he doesn't submit, slip your hand to his bicep and pin his arm to the mat. With your cradling arm, secure the wrist of the pinned arm. Maneuver the bottom man's arm into a position similar to the position of the head and arm while talking on the telephone. Once in place, switch grips and hyperextend your opponent's shoulder by sweeping his bent arm away from his head in a semi-circle.

DOUBLE WRISTLOCK AND SETUP FOR OUTSIDE TOEHOLD

From a front cross body position, force your opponent's arm to bend by driving your weight through your forearm and into his biceps. Secure his wrist and fold his arm into an acute angle at the elbow. Frame up your arms into the double wristlock position and sag backward, rolling your opponent toward you and onto his side. Push his wrist away from his back for the submission (not shown: for added pressure, take your knee that is nearest to his head and pin his head down as you apply the submission). If the bottom man attempts to bridge out from underneath, abandon the double wristlock and reach for his outside toe. Torque his knee joint by pulling his toes while pushing his shin with your forearm.

KARL GOTCH TOEHOLD TO FRANK GOTCH TOEHOLD COMBINATION

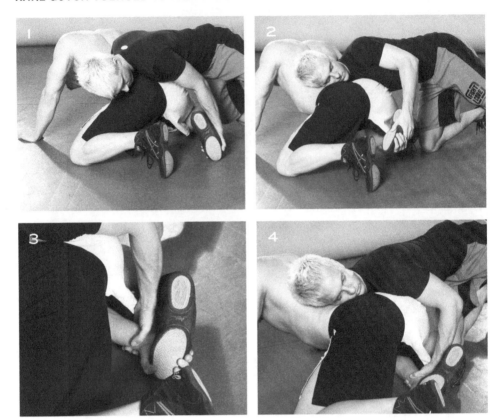

From the rear cross body position with the bottom man taking a high defensive position, grab your opponent's near-side foot at the toes. Reach your other hand deep inside and pass his foot from one hand to the other. Once secured, frame up your hands with your wrist against his near-side ankle and take the submission. If your opponent happens to kick his near-side leg free, immediately transition to attacking his far-side ankle. Grabbing his far-side ankle, drop your shoulder and drive the bottom man over onto his side. Landing on your opponent's leg, maintain a firm grip and pin his ankle while grabbing his toes with your other hand. Push your opponent's toes toward his head to take the submission.

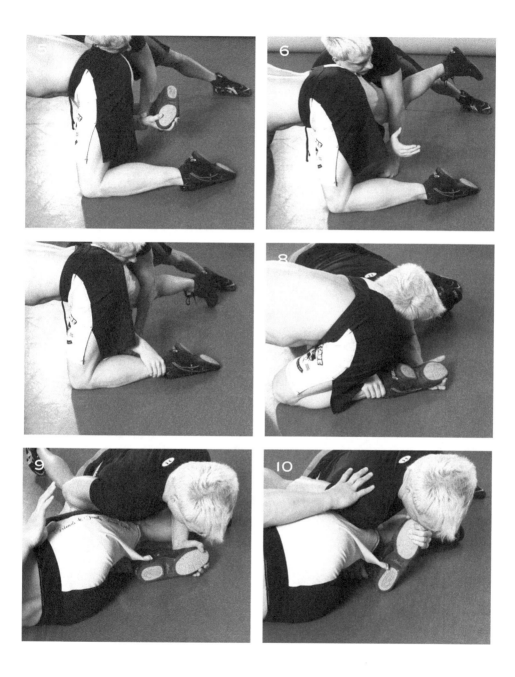

FURTHER NELSON PIN/SUBMISSION

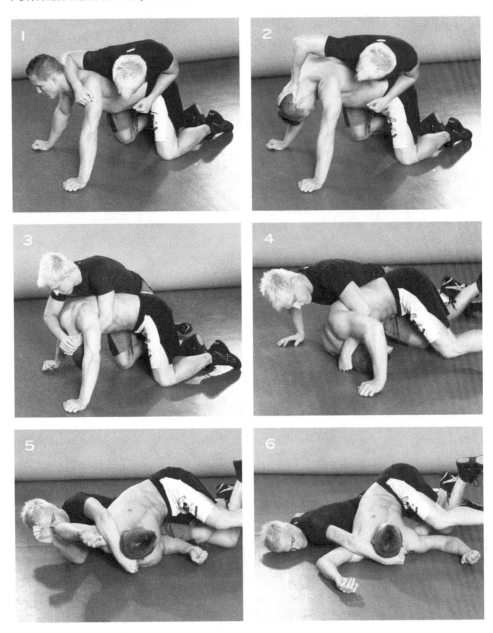

From a side ride, push your opponent's head down and secure a nelson with the opponent's far arm. As you break your man down, flatten your own body. Since you have grapevined the near-side leg with the side ride position, applying the further nelson wrings your opponent out like a rag. The further nelson is similar to the wrestler's guillotine (a.k.a. the twister) pin/submission.

KARL GOTCH'S RULES FOR MODERN CATCH WRESTLING

This is the rule set Karl suggested to me when I devised and promoted the first ever King of Catch Wrestling tournaments.

1. Submission or pin wins. All submissions are permitted and the pin count is three (both scapulae must be touching for the full three-count by the referee). Slamming and strangles allowed.
2. All matches are best two out of three falls.
3. Win, lose, or draw. No point system is used to determine the final outcome. In the event of a draw during tournament play, a rematch is played. In the event of a second draw, both wrestlers will be eliminated.
4. Twelve-minute time limit per fall with one minute of rest between falls.
5. All matches occur in a ring or on mat. While any body part on the ropes or out of bounds can break the action, such a break is entirely at the referee's discretion. (This discretionary measure is included to prevent the aggressive wrestler from being punished and to prevent the passive wrestler from stalling and forcing resets by intentionally going out of bounds.)
6. All referee-mandated resets start the opponents in the center of the wrestling area, with the offending wrestler in the down-low defensive position.
7. No striking, biting, eye gouging, or hair pulling. Instant disqualification.
8. Divisions include:
   - ★ Super heavyweight (over 225 pounds/102 kg)
   - ★ Heavyweight (over 200 pounds/91 kg)
   - ★ Light heavyweight (180 pounds/82 kg)
   - ★ Middleweight (160 pounds/73 kg)
   - ★ Lightweight (140 pounds/64 kg)
   - ★ Open

★ ★ ★ CONCLUSION ★ ★ ★

I CANNOT IMPROVE ON "FARMER" BURNS'S advice on how to begin as a catch wrestler, so I will simply let you read it for yourself. This is from his *Lessons in Wrestling and Physical Culture,* Book II[29]:

> FIRST: Study the pictures and the *names of each hold* until you are thoroughly familiar with it. This is necessary for we refer to the holds very frequently throughout the course, and you must know exactly what we mean when we say "half-Nelson," "grape-vine," "chancery," "scissor hold," etc. There are many, many holds to come later, so learn them thoroughly as we go.
>
> SECOND: With the assistance of a companion, take these holds one after another until you are entirely familiar with the positions of the entire body when the hold is in force. Remember that the *entire body* must be in the right position. Every angle must be *strong*, for a good hold is useless unless backed up with forceful angles of the body, the feet, arms, neck, shoulders and legs.
>
> *Caution*—Do not try to do much wrestling at first. Do not use these holds on your companion to the extent of

---

29 http://www.sandowplus.co.uk/Competition/Burns/lessons/lesson02.htm

hurting him. Simply practice the holds in order to become familiar with them. The real work will come later.

THIRD: Have your companion take various holds *on you*, to accustom yourself to them. Study the pictures. Let your companion take the holds *firmly*. You may then try to break the holds, but do not try too hard at first. Simply *resist*, for resistance is the basis of all physical culture. It is just as important for you to be able to *resist* the opponent's hold as it is for you to apply them successfully, for in a real contest your opponent is also trained, and you will change from the aggressor to the defensive many times in an evenly balanced match.

FOURTH: Lay the lesson aside and write a list of the holds. This is a splendid way to learn them. If you have time, write the name of each hold and then try to write a description of it. Try to make the description so plain that anyone could understand it without an illustration. This is merely a suggestion for those who have never wrestled and do not know the names of the usual wrestling holds. The amateur or professional will, of course, not find this necessary.

FIFTH: Farmer Burns says: "Practice these holds every day. You need not try to throw your companion or have him throw you, but secure the holds and *resist*. Push, pull and tug, that's what does the business. Work easy the first few days. Increase the efforts and power each time, and at the end of two weeks you will be twice as strong as you are now in the muscles used in this practice. *Be careful* with the hammerlock and other painful holds, yet put them on as far as you can stand them each time. You must be able to *resist all holds*, and the way to resist successfully is to train the muscles and harden them by *actual work*."

★ ★ ★ CATCH-AS-CATCH-CAN LEXICON ★ ★ ★

ACHILLES LOCK
An ankle submission created by compressing the Achilles tendon.

ANKLE RIDE
An attempt to control or break down your opponent's lower half by grasping and lifting his ankle.

ARM DRAG
Used as a takedown or a setup for a takedown and designed to move your opponent's arm. One of your arms acts as a guide arm, which moves your opponent's arm in the desired direction, while your other arm acts as a power arm, hooking his arm and moving it the rest of the way.

BACK ARCH
Arching backward from your feet to your head or shoulder to throw your opponent.

BEAR HUG

A move that involves locking your arms around your opponent's back while facing him. Be certain to get your hips tight to your opponent.

BEELL, FRED (1876–1933)

Native-born Wisconsin wrestler and one of the stars of wrestling's golden age. Beell's career peaked in 1906, when he defeated Frank Gotch for the American heavyweight catch-as-catch-can champion-ship. Although he was relatively short at 5 feet 7 (1.7 m) and never wrestled with more than a light heavyweight stature, Beell defeated many of the top wrestlers of the era, including Gotch and Baltimore standout Americus (Gus Schoenlein). His life ended tragically when, while working as a police officer, he was shot in the line of duty.

BIBBY, EDWIN (1848–?)

British-born Lancashire wrestler Edwin Bibby first made inroads into the North American professional wrestling scene in early 1881, wrest-ling world Greco-Roman wrestling champion William Muldoon in New York City. He is believed to be the first prominent Lancashire stylist to make a living in North America. He also helped pave the way for the American catch-as-catch-can wrestling style.

BODY SCISSOR

A move in which you lock legs around the body of your opponent and squeeze violently.

BOSTON CRAB

A move designed to create stress on your opponent's spine and stretch his abdomen. It involves sitting on your opponent's back and using one or both of his legs as levers.

BOTHNER, GEORGE (1867–1954)

A lightweight catch-as-catch-can wrestler, George Bothner was presented with the *Police Gazette* lightweight title belt in 1899. He claimed the world championship until his retirement in 1914. Later, Bothner owned a famous New York City gym, which bore his name.

BREAKDOWN

A move designed to break your opponent down to the mat on his side or stomach, off his base. It may lead to a ride or a pin.

BRIDGE

An arched position in which your back is facing the mat and you are pushing on your head, elbows, and feet so your shoulders are off of the mat.

BURNS, MARTIN "FARMER" (1861–1937)

Farmer Burns wrestled over 6,000 matches of every type and style, from grading camps to circuses. He lost only seven matches. He won the world wrestling title in 1895, when he defeated Evan "The Strangler" Lewis, and retained the title until 1897, when he was defeated by Tom Jenkins. He later won and held the light heavyweight title until 1908. Burns weighed only 175 pounds (80 kg) but defeated many of the great wrestlers of the day—some outweighing him by 50 to 100 pounds (23–46 kg). He had a very strong neck, which measured 20 inches (50 cm) and allowed him to perform one of his favorite stunts, a six-foot (1.8-m) hangman's drop, which he performed many times.

CADDOCK, EARL CHARLIE (1888–1950)

Iowa wrestler Earl Charlie Caddock first gained fame as an AAU wrestling champion and later, in 1917, as world heavyweight champion, handing Joe Stecher his first loss in the process. Like McLeod and Beell before him, Caddock held his own and defeated much larger heavyweights. Unfortunately, Caddock's career was severely hampered when he was gassed during service in World War I.

CARDINAL, DICK (1927–)

Cardinal started wrestling professionally in 1949, with Western Shows, and is a former carnival wrestler, with the Athletic Show. He began wrestling in YMCA programs and later learned catch-as-catch-can from Estonian-born shooter August Sepp Vic Short. He is considered one of the few remaining experts in the art of catch-as-catch-can.

CATCH-AS-CATCH-CAN

A set of rules for wrestling that was particularly popular in the late 19th century and early 20th century. The stranglehold is often barred, and a win is determined via a pin or concession hold. Most professional matches were decided with the best two of three bouts.

CHAIN WRESTLING

Performing maneuvers in combination when an initial maneuver doesn't work. It requires the use of holds that blend together, either as a fake to set up or as a follow-up to a missed hold or submission.

CORNWALL-AND-DEVONSHIRE STYLE

A set of jacketed wrestling rules in which the aim is to throw the opponent while, like in judo, grabbing onto his harness or jacket. It is named after the English counties where it was developed. Early forms, particularly the Devonshire style, allowed combatants to wear, and kick each other with, steel-toed boots.

CRADLE

A controlling position that involves holding your opponent from behind with one arm under one of his knees and the other around his head. There are many variations.

CROOKED HEAD SCISSOR

A punishing hold in which the opponent's neck is caught between your knees.

CROSS FACE

The act of placing the bony part of your forearm across your opponent's face in order to drive his head to the side.

DOUBLE WRISTLOCK

A submission hold in which you hold your opponent's wrist, bend his arm downward, and frame up with your other arm. Often called a *kimura* in Brazilian jujitsu.

ESCAPE

A move in which one wrestler breaks free of the other wrestler's control.

FULL NELSON

A punishing hold in which you reach under both of your opponent's arms from across his back and brace your hands on his head.

FURTHER NELSON

A half nelson in which you apply the hold to your opponent's further arm as opposed to his near-side arm. Thus, if you are to your opponent's left flank you would apply a further nelson to his right side.

FLYING MARE

This throw is usually performed by putting your weight on your opponent's upper body then pivoting 180 degrees, so you are both facing the same direction and your shoulder is under his same-side shoulder. From this position, you hold tight to your opponent, drop your weight to your knees, and hurl him over your body.

GORDIENKO, GEORGE (1928–2002)

Arguably the most proficient Canadian professional wrestler in recent history, Gordienko trained with the legendary Joe Pazandak and was managed by Tony Stecher early on. Many believe his wrestling career in the United States was severely hampered by McCarthyism. Gordienko turned to painting in his later years, becoming a well-respected artist whose works command prices as high as $30,000.

GOTCH, FRANK (1878–1917)

Considered one of the greatest in the history of the sport, Gotch was trained by "Farmer" Burns and made his first run at the big time when he challenged Tom Jenkins for the American championship in 1903. His lack of experience was evident, and Jenkins easily defeated him. However, Gotch secured the championship from Jenkins one year later and began a title reign that would last for over eight years.

GOTCH, KARL (1924–2007)

Known in Japan as the "God of Pro Wrestling," Karl Gotch is a legendary hooker and competitor. He wrestled for Belgium in the 1948 Olympics and later trained at Billy Riley's Snake Pit.

GOUGING (ROUGH AND TUMBLE)

The act of attacking an opponent's soft and hard targets in order to inflict pain and maximize discomfort. Gouging can be used to set up holds or to outright maim the opponent.

GO-BEHIND

The act of getting behind your opponent and controlling him.

GRAPEVINE

When you have one or both of your opponent's legs wrapped up with your legs.

GRECO-ROMAN WRESTLING

A traditional international form of wrestling whose modern form was born in France. Wrestlers may use only their arms and upper bodies and may only attack or hold their opponents above the waist and higher.

GRUBMEYER, FRED (1886–1978)

Also known as the "Iowa Cornstalk," Grubmeyer wrestled professionally throughout the United States and Canada. He also "barnstormed," playing the role of a rube to hustle betting money out of locals. Despite possessing an awkward and gangly build, Grubmeyer was a clever and incredibly skilled wrestler who was well-liked by fans and respected by his peers.

HACKENSCHMIDT, GEORGE (1877–1968)

A world champion Greco-Roman and catch-as-catch-can wrestler, Hackenschmidt is also known as the "Russian Lion." He ranks along with Tom Jenkins and Frank Gotch as one of the greatest catch-as-catch-can wrestlers in history. He also held several weight-lifting records and wrote extensively on the subject of physical culture.

HALF NELSON

A hold in which you generate enormous leverage by inserting your left arm under your opponent's left arm from his left side (or your right arm from your opponents right side). You then force your opponent's head down and pull it toward you while raising his left shoulder so he rolls over to the right (or raise his right shoulder so he rolls to the left) and lies on his back. This hold can also be executed with the legs.

HAMMERLOCK

A hold in which you pull your opponent's arm behind his back and bend it up and away from his back.

HEAD CHANCERY

Any position in which an attacking wrestler holds a defending wrestler's head and neck. Head chancery is a shortened way of saying "head in chancery" ("in chancery" means in a hopeless situation). The term head chancery typically refers to variations of the front and side head-lock, but it has also been used to indicate other types of choke holds, strangles, and neck cranks.

HEADLOCK

A hold in which the head of one wrestler is encircled and locked by the arm and body of the other wrestler.

JENKINS, TOM (1873–1957)

Having won against the likes of Frank Gotch and Farmer Burns, Jenkins was known to be a very tough heavyweight wrestler who used his rough and calloused hands to rip his opponents' flesh. With only one eye and a reputation for being very game, he was known as "America's Wrestling Champion." After retiring from wrestling he was appointed by U.S. President Theodore Roosevelt as the head self-defense coach at the Military Academy at West Point.

LONDOS, JIM (1897–1975)

Greek-born immigrant and bodybuilder whose wrestling name was inspired by popular author Jack London. During the 1920s and 1930s, Londos was the top box-office draw in wrestling. Though some today dismiss his abilities as a wrestler, Londos was a legitimately talented catch-as-catch-can practitioner.

NECK CRANK

Any hold that a wrestler uses to attack his opponent by twisting then compressing the vertebrae of his neck.

OVER HOOK

Bringing your arm over your opponent's arm to gain control of that arm.

PUMMEL

The act of wrestling for inside hand position while in an upper body clinch.

QUARTER NELSON

A hold applied by threading, say, your left hand under your opponent's near shoulder, which means you are operating from his right side. Your right hand then bears down on the back of your opponent's neck while you grip your own right wrist with your left hand. Your right hand then presses heavily against your victim's neck and head as high up as possible.

RIDE

This is the act of dominating and controlling your opponent. It precedes a pin or concession hold.

RILEY, BILLY (1896–1977)

An accomplished Lancashire-style catch-as-catch-can wrestler, Riley won the British Empire Championship from Jack Robinson in Africa, breaking Robinson's arm in the process. Riley established the feared and respected Snake Pit wrestling gym in Wigan, England, where such notable wrestlers as Karl Gotch, Billy Robinson, Bert Azzeratti, and Billy Joyce trained.

ROBINSON, BILLY (1939–)

An accomplished British wrestler and AWA British Empire champion, Robinson trained under Billy Joyce (a.k.a. Bob Robinson) at Billy Riley's Snake Pit gym. When Robinson won the Commonwealth Games title in England as an amateur, George Hackenschmidt gave him the award. He has more recently been coaching mixed martial artists, including Kazushi Sakuraba and Josh Barnett, in Japan and the United States.

SALTO
A takedown in which you arch your back and toss your opponent overhead.

SATURDAY NIGHT RIDE
A ride in which the top wrestler is between the legs of the bottom wrestler, in a bottom body scissor.

SCRAMBLE
A race between wrestlers to establish dominance.

SHOOT
In amateur wrestling, shooting refers to what was known to old-timers as a leg dive. In professional wrestling, a shoot refers to a legitimate contest.

SHOOTER
A catch-as-catch-can term for a skilled and accomplished wrestler. A shooter has a broad base of knowledge in all areas of the art of catch wrestling.

SHORT ARM SCISSOR
A hold in which you insert your arm into the joint of your opponent's elbow. You then lever down to compress your opponent's elbow joint, typically using your leg to apply downward pressure.

SIT-OUT
A fundamental mat wrestling technique that allows you to move your hips away from your opponent while trying to escape or reverse.

SNAP DOWN
A takedown commonly used from an inside tie-up. You pull your opponent's head downward sharply and use his forward momentum to help you bring him to the mat.

SPRAWL

The act of bringing your hips violently downward by throwing your legs back. The sprawl is a fundamental wrestling maneuver with many applications. Typically, it is used from a standing position to stop an opponent's shot. In catch-as-catch-can, it is also often used to enable an escape or as a way of turning a hold into a hook.

STECHER, JOE (1893–1974)

Aptly nicknamed the "Scissor King" for his adept use of the body scissors, Joe Stecher was the dominant heavyweight wrestler in the period directly following Frank Gotch's retirement. He first held the world heavyweight title between 1915 and 1917, the latter date marking the first fall that was ever scored against him during his professional career. Stecher remained a major force in wrestling for the next 10 years, claiming the world's title on several occasions.

STOPPER TOEHOLD

A type of twisting ankle lock in which you figure-four your arms around your opponent's ankle, usually grabbing the opponent's foot at the instep.

SWITCH

A technique that is commonly performed to counter a rear waist hold. You lever your arm against your opponent's arm, typically by reaching back and grabbing his inner thigh while trapping his arm. At the same time, you move your hips away from him in order to allow for a reversal or an escape.

THREE-QUARTER NELSON

A hold in which you apply the nelson to the near side of your opponent by using both of your hands. If you are to his right flank you reach under his right arm with your right arm until your hand rests on the back of his head. Your left arm then snakes under your opponent's right arm and head and comes up to meet your right hand from the opposite side.

TOP WRISTLOCK (THE JAPANESE WRISTLOCK)

A submission hold in which you bend your opponent's arm upward at the elbow and, optimally, attack your opponent's wrist, elbow, and shoulder joint simultaneously.

TRIP

A takedown in which you attack your opponent's foot or leg with your foot or leg, typically pushing in the opposite direction.

UNDER HOOK

Bringing your arm under your opponent's arm in order to gain control of that arm.

WHIZZER (THE HANK)

This single over hook is used to control the opponent. It can be used in a myriad of situations, such as setting up upper body takedowns, as a counter to the opponent's takedown attempts, or as a means of escape.